Bala Shanmugam
Monash University

Zaha Rina Zahari
RBS Coutts

A Primer on
Islamic Finance

RESEARCH FOUNDATION
OF CFA INSTITUTE

Statement of Purpose

The Research Foundation of CFA Institute is a
not-for-profit organization established to promote
the development and dissemination of relevant
research for investment practitioners worldwide.

ISBN 978-1-934667-24-8

4 December 2009

Editorial Staff

Elizabeth Collins
Book Editor

David L. Hess
Assistant Editor

Cindy Maisannes
Publishing Technology Specialist

Lois Carrier
Production Specialist

Biographies

Bala Shanmugam is the chair of accounting and finance and director of banking and finance at the School of Business, Monash University Sunway campus, Malaysia. Professor Shanmugam is on the editorial boards of a number of reputed journals in the areas of banking and finance. He has extensive industry experience and has served as consultant to a number of financial institutions, including the World Bank. Author of more than 100 papers and 30 books, Professor Shanmugam has received many prestigious awards for his research and scholarship. He has presented papers at more than 40 conferences around the world and is a common figure in media appearances and citations. Professor Shanmugam obtained his PhD in banking and finance in Australia.

Zaha Rina Zahari works for the Royal Bank of Scotland Group as senior vice president of RBS Coutts, Singapore. Previously, Dr. Zahari served as CEO of RHB Securities. Prior to that, she was head of exchanges at Bursa Malaysia (previously KLSE), where she was responsible for overseeing securities (KLSE), offshore (Labuan FX), and high-technology growth companies (MESDAQ). Dr. Zahari also served as chief operating officer of the Malaysian Derivatives Exchange, and she started her career heading a leading futures brokerage firm, Sri Comm Options and Financial Futures. She is on the Global Board of Advisors at XBRL International, is a member of the board of trustees for the Malaysian AIDS Foundation, and is a regular speaker at major financial conferences. Dr. Zahari obtained her doctorate of business administration from Hull University, United Kingdom.

Contents

CFA Institute
CE Qualified Activity

This publication qualifies for 5 CE credits under the guidelines of the CFA Institute Continuing Education Program.

Foreword

Economics generally makes the assumption that human behavior is rational and, therefore, takes rationality as given. Religion, in contrast, considers humans to be fallible (thus potentially irrational) and aims to influence our behavior. Bringing religion into our economic lives, then, necessarily means bringing moral values into what is supposed to be free of such values. Some would think that never the twain—religion and economics—shall meet, but in reality, they do.

Moral values, often derived from the major religions of the world, are increasingly being introduced into our economic lives in the form of environmental concerns, protection of the rights of labor, and promotion of fairness in trade. In finance, the increased level of interest in socially responsible investments is a good case in point. It is in Islamic finance, however, where economics and religion really come together.

The rise of modern Islamic finance in various parts of the world has motivated many, whether academics or practitioners, to understand it. Investment professionals, including CFA charterholders, are no exception; they want to learn about Islamic finance because they are working in this industry, are considering joining it, or simply want to quench their intellectual thirst. Not surprisingly, many books have been written on Islamic finance to meet this demand, but there is a scarcity of introductory texts that are simple but comprehensive. This monograph is one such text—reader friendly and wide in scope: It covers basic Islamic financial concepts (such as *riba* and *gharar*), markets (banking, capital markets, insurance), products (bank accounts, equity funds, and *sukuk*), and issues, such as corporate governance and risk management. In presenting the material, the authors, Zaha Rina Zahari and Bala Shanmugam, with the assistance of principal researcher Lokesh Gupta, have made extensive use of the experience of their home country, Malaysia, which is perceived as the most advanced and liberal model of modern Islamic finance.

This monograph helps the reader understand that the Islamic finance industry does not have global *Shari'a* standards to decide what is and isn't compliant in every part of the world. Moreover, many observers note that there is a gap between the theory of Islamic finance and its practice; they argue that the industry is putting form over substance to merely replicate conventional financial products. The debate evokes much passion, and it seems to be gaining momentum as Islamic finance gains market share and attention.

But debate is an inevitable consequence of the merger of faith and finance and, in particular, of the emergence of Islamic finance. In the current global financial crisis, the intellectual environment seems to have become more conducive to considering alternative methods of meeting financial needs and increasing the role of moral values in our economic lives. This monograph is, therefore, in tune with the times. The Research Foundation of CFA Institute is pleased to present *A Primer on Islamic Finance*.

Usman Hayat, CFA
Director, Islamic Finance and ESG Investing
CFA Institute

Chapter 1. Overview of Contemporary Islamic Finance

The basic principles underlying Islamic financial transactions are that the purpose of financing should not involve an activity prohibited by *Shari'a* (Islamic law) and that the financing must not involve *riba* (the giving or receiving of interest) and should avoid *gharar* (uncertainty, risk, and speculation). For instance, because gambling is against *Shari'a*, any arrangement to finance a casino would always be against *Shari'a*. *Riba* and *gharar* will be explained at length later. At this point, the main aspect is that *riba* includes interest charged on lending money whereas *gharar* includes excessive uncertainty regarding essential elements of a contract, such as price in a contract of sale.

Islamic finance promotes the sharing of risk and reward between contracting parties. The degree of sharing varies by contract. An example of financing that involves a relatively high degree of risk-and-reward sharing is venture capital; a contract that has a relatively low degree of risk-and-reward sharing is sale of an asset on installment credit. The financier assumes either the risk of the outcome of the business or the risk of ownership of an asset before it is sold. Neither risk is assumed in money lending, where the main risk assumed by the financier is credit risk—that is, the risk that the one being financed will lack the ability or the willingness to pay the money owed. Credit risk is also present in installment credit sales, but it is in addition to, not in substitution of, ownership risk.

Contemporary Islamic finance incorporates these principles and the other doctrines of the Muslim faith in a wide variety of products to meet the growing global demand for *Shari'a*-compliant investment and financing. The spread of Islamic financial principles is supported by the fact that Islam permits the accumulation of wealth as long as the source of wealth generation does not breach Islamic principles (that is, the activities are *halal*, or permissible),[1] *zakat* (a religious tithe) is paid, and wastefulness is avoided.

Origins of Islamic Banking and Finance

Collins (1881) described the origin of banking as "beyond the range of authentic history" (p. 11). According to Collins, banking may be assumed to have emerged as a necessary outgrowth of commerce. The notion of a medium of exchange was born because of the inconvenience of meeting and matching in barter trade, which commenced as civilizations evolved, and because people's needs increased and

---

[1]The statement on the permissibility of the accumulation of wealth can be found in "Islamic Capital Market Review" (2005).

self-sufficiency declined. Because the mighty institution of banking arose after the establishment of an appropriate medium of exchange, the next logical and sequential step in the process was the development of the activities of lending and borrowing.

The first banks are believed to have originated within the temples of the ancient religions of the cultures encircling the Mediterranean Sea. In these temples, the priests and moneylenders conducted transactions and accepted deposits in what is believed to be the first currency, grain. Eventually, easier-to-carry precious metals replaced bulky grains as a means of exchange. In ancient Mesopotamia, in the area now known as Iran, evidence indicates that temples acted as the guardian places of official weights for measuring silver, the commonly used monetary medium in the region, and that records of payments, loans, and other transactions were kept in the temples.

The first stable international currency, the gold *bezant*, emerged in the fourth century and was coined by the Byzantine Empire, which bridged the medieval European and Islamic cultures through its capital in Constantinople, now called Istanbul (Grierson 1999). The availability of a widely recognized and cross-cultural currency enabled people to undertake more ambitious commercial ventures and wider travel than in the past and provided increased opportunities for private individuals to acquire wealth throughout Europe and the Middle East.

Following the emergence of stable coinage, banking activities quickly developed to accommodate international trade. Early merchant banks began to deal in bills of exchange and credit-based transactions. These new financing instruments eliminated the need for merchants to actually deliver the precious metals and coins to pay for transactions in distant ports.

In the 11th century, Western Europe, to finance the Crusades, revitalized its credit-based banking system. Thus, the combined forces of Middle Eastern and Western European banking practices were exported around the world as the nations of these regions undertook new global exploration and international trading relationships.

Nevertheless, Goitein (1971) asserted that partnership and profit-sharing financing structures—concepts that are integral to Islamic finance—continued to flourish in areas of the Mediterranean region as late as the 12th and 13th centuries. And they exist today around the world in the form of cooperatives (such as customer-owned retail or food stores), mutual *takaful* (Islamic insurance) companies, and others.

Emergence of Contemporary Islamic Finance

According to Iqbal and Molyneux (2005), partnerships and profit-sharing ventures consistent with the beliefs of Islam were commonly used to finance productive activities even prior to the teachings of the Prophet Muhammad. Over time, however, as the center of economic gravity moved to the Western world, the profit-sharing approach to structuring financial transactions fell out of favor and Western financial institutions came to dominate the capital markets. Islamic financial institutions gradually succumbed to the ways of the West and adopted interest-based financial transactions (Iqbal and Molyneux 2005). Infighting within the Muslim community contributed to the general acceptance of Western, or conventional, financing methods.[2]

The establishment of the Mit Ghamr Islamic Bank in Egypt in 1963 is often viewed as the starting point of the modern Islamic banking movement. Evidence exists, however, that interest-free commercial financial transactions existed in various parts of the Muslim world several decades earlier. For instance, the institution Anjuman Mowodul Ikhwan of Hyderabad, India, made interest-free loans to Muslims as early as the 1890s. Another institution in Hyderabad, the Anjuman Imdad-e-Bahmi Qardh Bila Sud, was established in 1923 by employees of the Department of Land Development and, within 20 years, had assets worth US$2,240 and was distributing loans of US$100 to US$135 per month. The bank had a membership of 1,000, which included Muslims and non-Muslims. By 1944, it had reserves of US$67,000. These organizations made small loans to small businesses on a profit-sharing basis. Their activities continue to this day.

In the early 1960s, the convergence of political and socioeconomic factors ignited interest in the revival of faith-based Islamic financial practices, including the prohibition of usury, or the giving or receiving of interest (*riba*). Although "usury" is commonly used today to mean an excessive rate of interest, it applies in this context to any charging of interest for the use of money. Islamic finance makes a distinction between usury and a "rate of return or profit from capital." Profit in a business venture is determined *ex post*—that is, *depending on the outcome of the venture*—in contrast to interest, which is determined *ex ante*—that is, *regardless of the outcome of the venture*. Profit in a trade or a sale may be determined *ex ante*, but it is based on trading real assets between contracting parties, not the lending of money on interest (Iqbal and Tsubota 2006).

Iqbal and Tsubota (2006) asserted that, although the prohibition of *riba* is the core of the Islamic financial system, the system's prevailing practices also reflect other principles and doctrines of Islam, such as the admonition to share profits, the promotion of entrepreneurship, the discouragement of speculative behavior, the preservation of property rights, transparency, and the sanctity of contractual obligations. The Islamic financial system "can be fully appreciated only in the context of Islam's teachings on the work ethic, wealth distribution, social and economic justice, and the expected responsibilities of the individual, society, the state, and all stakeholders" (p. 6).

---

[2]A different version of this history is told in some academic literature (notably Kuran 2004). This literature asserts that the basic principles of what is now known as Islamic finance were not followed in what Westerners call medieval times. Instead, Kuran says, what are now known as Islamic financial principles were first set forth by, among others, the Pakistani scholar Abul Ala Maududi (1903–1979). This monograph presumes that Islamic financial principles have an ancient origin.

Nevertheless, not all Muslims embrace Islamic finance with open arms. Efforts within the Islamic finance movements are being made to use *heyal* (ruses or deceptive practices) to circumvent *Shari'a*, as was done in other Abrahamic faiths; that is, from the Muslim perspective, followers of the Judeo-Christian religions have rejected similar admonitions to forswear usury.

Mahmoud Amin El-Gamal, who holds the Islamic finance chair at Rice University in Houston, Texas, claims that the Islamic finance industry is selling overpriced products to the religiously and financially naive and that some of the product differentiation between Islamic and conventional financial products appears to be hairsplitting. El-Gamal has said:

> Both the sophisticated investors and the ultra-puritans will see through this charade. So you're left with the gullible who don't really understand the structure. . . . Muslims around the world have among the worst rates of literacy. . . . Take that same money and give it to charity. (Quoted in Morais 2007)

The U.S. banker Muhammad Saleem made similar remarks critical of Islamic finance in his 2006 book *Islamic Banking: A $300 Billion Deception*.

Moreover, some have said that certain financing methods with *predetermined* markups, or profit margins, which are described in Chapter 4 (such as *bai' bithaman ajil* financing), have become a generally accepted part of Islamic finance even though these practices involve limited risk-and-reward sharing and thus resemble fixed-interest lending in significant ways.[3]

Basic Tenets of Islamic Finance

In contrast to the authors of these critiques, we believe that Islamic finance governed by the principles of *Shari'a* encompasses the ethos and value system of Islam. Primary tenets of Islamic finance are the avoidance of *riba* (interest), *gharar* (uncertainty, risk, and speculation), and *haram* (religiously prohibited) activities. Therefore, Islamic finance strictly prohibits interest-based transactions, but it embraces the sharing of profit and loss or, in other words, sharing of the risk by the provider and the user of the funds invested. The ownership and trading of a physical good or service is a critical element in structuring Islamic financial products.

Islamic finance encourages active participation of financial institutions and investors in achieving the goals and objectives of an Islamic economy. It merges the ethical teachings of Islam with finance as a means to meet the needs of society and to encourage socioeconomic justice. Through *haram*, Islamic finance prohibits trading in, for example, alcoholic beverages, gambling, and pork.

---

[3] Usman Hayat in a private communication with the authors.

The primary players in the Islamic financial system are Islamic banks and the Islamic "windows" of conventional, or Western, banks. An Islamic bank has been defined in the following ways:

- The general secretariat of the Organisation of the Islamic Conference, an association of 56 Islamic states promoting solidarity in economic, social, and political affairs, defines an Islamic bank as "a financial institution whose statutes, rules, and procedures expressly state its commitment to the principle of *Shari'a* and to the banning of the receipt and payment of interest on any of its operations" (Ali and Sarkar 1995, p. 22).

- The Malaysian Islamic Banking Act 1983 states that an Islamic bank is "any company which carries on Islamic banking business and holds a valid licence" (Part 1). Islamic banking business is further defined as that "whose aims and operations do not involve any element which is not approved by the Religion of Islam" (Part 1).

- The Central Bank Law of Kuwait (1968, as amended in 2003) stipulates that Islamic banks "exercise the activities pertaining to banking business and any activities considered by the Law of Commerce or by customary practice as banking activities in compliance with the Islamic *Shari'a* principles."[4]

Exhibit 1.1 summarizes the differences between conventional and Islamic banking.

Objectives of *Shari'a* in Islamic Finance

The objectives of *Shari'a* and the objectives of Islamic financial institutions may differ. If, however, industry practices are in line with the substance of *Shari'a*, they should lead to fulfillment of the objectives of *Shari'a*.

The principal objective of *Shari'a* as explained in literature on Islamic finance is economic justice through equitable distribution of resources. The rationale offered is quite simple. Lending money for interest directs the flow of money to those who are considered low credit risks (a government, for instance) or those who can provide collateral (say, a rich individual or a big company), even if they may not have the businesses and ideas with the greatest economic potential. Such behavior, it is argued, leads to such economic ills as the concentration of wealth in a few hands, which, in turn, have wide social implications.

The objective of Islamic financial institutions is the pursuit of profits without violating *Shari'a*. The shareholders of and investors in Islamic financial institutions

---

[4]The original law may be found at www.cbk.gov.kw/www/law.html; the amended law is at www.cbk.gov.kw/PDF/Stat-Law-amend.PDF.

Exhibit 1.1. Comparison of Islamic and Conventional Banking

Characteristic	Islamic Banking System	Conventional Banking System (interest based)
Business framework	Functions and operating modes are based on *Shari'a*, and Islamic banks must ensure that all business activities are in compliance with *Shari'a* requirements.	Functions and operating modes are based on secular principles, not religious laws or guidelines.
Interest charging	Financing is not interest (*riba*) oriented and should be based on risk-and-reward sharing.	Financing is interest oriented, and a fixed or variable interest rate is charged for the use of money.
Interest on deposits	Account holders do not receive interest (*riba*) but may share risk and rewards of investments made by the Islamic bank.	Depositors receive interest and a guarantee of principal repayment.
Risk sharing in equity financing	Islamic banks offer equity financing with risk sharing for a project or venture. Losses are shared on the basis of the equity participation, whereas profit is shared on the basis of a pre-agreed ratio.	Risk sharing is not generally offered but is available through venture capital firms and investment banks, which may also participate in management.
Restrictions	Islamic banks are allowed to participate only in economic activities that are *Shari'a* compliant. For example, banks cannot finance a business that involves selling pork or alcohol.	Conventional banks may finance any lawful product or service.
Zakat (religious tax)	One of the functions of the Islamic banks is to collect and distribute *zakat*.	Conventional banks do not collect any religious tax.
Penalty on default	Islamic banks are not allowed to charge penalties for their enrichment. They may, however, allow imposition of default or late-payment penalties on the grounds that these penalties discourage late payments or defaults, which impose administrative costs on banks for processing and collecting the amount owed. Penalties may be donated to a charity or used to offset collection costs.	Conventional banks normally charge additional money (compound interest) in case of late payments or defaults.
Avoidance of *gharar*	Transactions with elements of gambling or speculation are discouraged or forbidden.	Speculative investments are allowed.
Customer relationships	The status of an Islamic bank in relation to its clients is that of partner and investor.	The status of a conventional bank in relation to its clients is one of creditor and debtor.
Shari'a supervisory board	Each Islamic bank must have a supervisory board to ensure that all its business activities are in line with *Shari'a* requirements.	Conventional banks have no such requirement.
Statutory requirements	An Islamic bank must be in compliance with the statutory requirements of the central bank of the country in which it operates and also with *Shari'a* guidelines.	A conventional bank must be in compliance with the statutory requirements of the central bank of the country in which it operates and in some places, the banking laws of state or other localities.

may have purely economic considerations and not be concerned with the objectives of *Shari'a*. Among the most important policies or goals pursued by the Islamic financial system are the following:

- **Shari'a-compliant financial products and services.** To be *Shari'a* compliant, the financial products and services must not be based on the payment or receipt of interest. Kuran (2004) quotes the Islamic economist Afzalur Rahman as saying that interest "inculcates love for money and the desire to accumulate wealth for its own sake. It makes men selfish, miserly, narrow-minded, and stonehearted" (p. 8). This view corresponds roughly to the persona of the money lender Shylock in Shakespeare's *The Merchant of Venice*. Indeed, literature in various cultures, including South Asia, portrays individual money lenders in a negative light. Not surprisingly, "usurer" has particularly negative connotations.

- **Stability in money value.** Stability in the value of money is believed to be enhanced by requiring that currency be backed by an underlying asset, which enables the medium of exchange to be a reliable unit of account. Islam recognizes money as a store of wealth and as a means of exchange but does not view money as a commodity that should be bought and sold at a profit (Ismail 2005).

- **Economic development.** Participatory-type financing for infrastructure projects, based on *mudharabah* (profit sharing) and *musyarakah* (joint venture), is designed so that investment returns to both the provider and the user of funds will reflect the success of the project. The mechanism of sharing profits leads to a close working relationship between bank and entrepreneur and is believed to encourage economic development as a result of the bank's equity-type stake in the financed project (versus an interest-only or fixed profit potential).

- **Social development.** *Zakat* (a religious tithe) is paid by Muslims and deposited into a fund that is distributed to the poor directly or through religious institutions. *Zakat* is imposed at a rate roughly equivalent to 2.5 percent of the market value of an individual's real and financial property. *Zakat* may also be imposed on the initial capital of an Islamic bank, its reserves, and its profits. *Zakat* is one of the five main pillars of Islam and is one of the most significant manifestations of social solidarity in Islam. The understanding is that social welfare and development of the poor are improved through the collection of *zakat*.

- **Resource optimization.** Funding is provided only for projects that, in the bank's estimate, have the most favorable return-for-risk forecasts, in addition to meeting the criterion of being socially beneficial. Projects are selected primarily on the basis of their anticipated profitability rather than the creditworthiness of the borrower (Al-Omar and Abdel-Haq 1996).

- **Equitable distribution of resources.** One of the aims of Islamic banking is to serve the less fortunate by promoting the equitable distribution of resources. The distribution of income and resources of Islamic financial structures is intended to be proportionate to the value offered by participating parties.

Principles of Islamic Finance

Islamic finance is based on the themes of community banking, ethical banking, and socially responsible investing. Its goal is to be an ethical, indigenous, and equitable mode of finance. The five key principles that govern Islamic finance are as follows.

Freedom from *Riba*. *Riba* is Arabic for "growth" or "increase" and denotes the payment or receipt of interest for the use of money. The Quran, the Muslim holy book, expressly forbids *riba*, which includes any payment of interest (not only excessive interest) on monetary loans. The Quran states, "O You who believe! Fear Allah and give up what remains of your demand for usury, if you are indeed believers." (Recall the previous comment that in its traditional definition, "usury" encompasses *any* payment of interest.) Muslim scholars have interpreted *riba* to mean any fixed or guaranteed interest payment on cash advances or on deposits (Mahmood 2004).

In prohibiting *riba*, Islam seeks to foster an environment based on fairness and justice. A loan with a fixed return to the lender regardless of the outcome of the borrower's course of action is viewed as unfair. *Riba* is also believed to be exploitative and unproductive because it is considered to represent sure gain to the lender without any possibility of loss as well as a reward in return for no work. These factors are believed to lead, in turn, to inflation and unemployment and to stifle the social and infrastructural development of a nation.

Risk-and-Return Sharing. *Shari'a* prohibits Muslims from earning income by charging interest but permits income generation through the sharing of risks and rewards (*mudharabah*) between the parties to a transaction. This profit-sharing mechanism is believed to encourage people to become partners and work together rather than to enter into a creditor–debtor relationship. Partnership promotes mutual responsibility for the outcome of the financed project, which is believed to increase the likelihood of success of the venture. A tangential aim of the partnership approach is that such increases in successful projects also provide stimulus to the economy.

Shari'a-Approved Activities. Islamic banks may engage in or finance only activities that do not violate the rules of *Shari'a* and are permitted by Islam. To ensure that all products and services offered are *Shari'a* compliant, each Islamic bank has an independent *Shari'a* supervisory board.

Sanctity of Contract. Islam views contractual obligations and the related full disclosure of information as a sacred duty. Full disclosure is intended to reduce financial speculation (*gharar*), which is strictly prohibited by Islam, by providing as much information as possible for investors to make accurate assessments about the risks and rewards of an investment. The conditions that are necessary for a contract to be valid include a competent understanding of the underlying asset(s) and the profit-sharing ratio, as well as the presence of a willing buyer and seller. Contracts must also not offend Islamic religious and moral principles; if they do, they will be deemed illegal and unenforceable.

Avoidance of *Gharar*. *Shari'a* prohibits financial transactions that involve *gharar*, which is often translated as "deception," "excessive risk," or "excessive uncertainty." Examples of *gharar* are the sale of fish in the sea, of birds in the sky, and of unripe fruits on the tree, which cause excessive and avoidable uncertainty.

Unlike *riba*, which involves the question of the presence or absence of interest, *gharar* raises the question of degree. And it does not apply to noncommutative contracts (i.e., those, such as gifts, that do not involve an exchange). It is not as well defined as *riba*, and a ruling of permissibility based on *gharar* could take into account a cost–benefit analysis. For instance, *gharar* is present in contracts where the object of the sale is not in the possession of the seller or does not exist at the time the parties enter into the contract but such contracts are permissible.

To minimize *gharar*, contracts must carefully state the terms of the agreement, particularly by giving a thorough description of the asset that is the subject of the contract and the asset's transaction price. In a sale, if the asset being sold and its price are not clearly defined or specified, the sale contract would be considered to have excessive *gharar*.[5]

Forces Strengthening Islamic Finance

A number of forces have combined recently to cause Islamic finance to grow sharply.

Transnational bodies have been established to overcome the challenges faced by Islamic finance. For example, the Islamic Financial Services Board and the Accounting and Auditing Organization for Islamic Financial Institutions have been established to standardize, respectively, practices and accounting policies for Islamic financial institutions. They have succeeded in eliminating or at least minimizing many of the obstacles facing the Islamic financial system, thereby enhancing its growth.

The skill level of Islamic bankers and other Islamic capital market participants has steadily improved through greater intrabank (Islamic) and interbank (conventional) competition. Market competition has also spurred the creation of new product structures to satisfy client demands. Such progress is an essential factor in the continued development and sustainability of the Islamic financial system.

The general deregulation of the global banking sector has also assisted Islamic banking by making room for the implementation of new ideas and allowing flexibility within the system. Hence, establishing new Islamic banks (or, at least, Islamic windows in conventional banks) has been relatively easy in, for example, Southeast Asia.

Globalization has also played an important part in the growth of the Islamic financial system. Globalization has resulted in increased opportunities for Muslim countries to assist and cooperate with one another in the development of an Islamic banking system and capital market. An excellent example is the growth in the *sukuk*

---

[5] See also El-Gamal (2006), pp. 58–59.

(Islamic bonds) market. Currently, much discussion surrounds the possibility of establishing an international Islamic interbank market to cater to the liquidity needs of Islamic banks.

Finally, information technology (IT), as well as facilitating banking operations, has greatly helped in disseminating information to clients, capital markets, and investors. As in conventional banking and finance, the use of IT has greatly reduced the cost of operations for Islamic financial institutions and improved the convenience of banking operations for bankers and customers. Thanks to IT, data and information on Islamic finance can now be obtained in real time from various sources for free or at a low cost. This development has allowed more and more people to understand and use Islamic finance.

Exhibit 1.2 summarizes these drivers and lists other drivers of growth in Islamic finance in recent years.

Exhibit 1.2. Drivers of Growth in Islamic Finance

Economic growth and liquidity	• Strengthened oil prices • Solid economic growth in the Gulf Cooperation Council (GCC) • Increased wealth being retained in the region as investment opportunities improve • Increased government spending and investment in infrastructure/development projects
Investor appetite for *Shari'a*-compliant instruments	• *Shari'a*-compliant instruments becoming increasingly popular with investors • Testified to by rapid emergence of *sukuk* (Islamic bonds) • Increase in desire of family enterprises to tap liquidity in order to go public
Privatization and foreign direct investment (FDI)	• Increased GCC privatization initiatives accelerating project finance and structured finance activity • Strong and improving FDI potential in the region because of rising sovereign ratings and human development
Regulatory changes	• Improving regulatory infrastructure • Liberalization of country markets and increased investor friendliness • Increased foreign participation
Diversification	• Movement of GCC countries' investments into nonoil sectors • Investor funds diversifying regionally throughout the GCC and greater Middle East region
Globalization	• Islamic financial instruments increasingly accepted globally because of globalization • Foreign regulators (e.g., in United States, United Kingdom, European Union, Canada, and Singapore) accepting Islamic finance • Entry of global players in Islamic finance

Note: The GCC consists of Bahrain, Kuwait, Oman, Qatar, Saudi Arabia, and the United Arab Emirates.
Source: Dauphine (2007).

Chapter 2. Islamic Law and Financial Services

Shari'a, Islamic religious law, forms the foundation of Islamic finance. *Shari'a* attempts to promote equality and fairness in society by emphasizing moral, social, ethical, and religious factors. This chapter covers the relationship between *Shari'a* and Islamic finance.

In general, Islamic finance refers to financial market transactions, operations, and services that comply with Islamic rules, principles, and codes of practice. In other words, Islamic finance is that which is guided by the ethos and value system of Islam. The goal of Islamic finance is to stress risk and reward sharing over exploitation, community well-being over materialism, and the brotherhood of humankind over the fragmentation of society.

Shari'a is not the law of the land, even in countries where Muslims make up a majority of the citizens. It is a body of religious law, aspects of which are incorporated into some countries' legal systems.

The Islamic Faith: Foundation of Islamic Law

The word "Islam" is derived from the word "*salaam*," which means submission or peace. A person who believes in and consciously follows Islam is a Muslim, a word that also comes from the same root of *salaam* (Khir, Gupta, and Shanmugam 2007). *Shari'a*, or the divine law in Islam, is based on the Quran and the *Sunnah*, the reported sayings of the Prophet Muhammad.

Figure 2.1 and **Figure 2.2** illustrate how *Shari'a* embraces most aspects of a Muslim's life—worship, personal attitude and conduct, social norms, politics, economic conventions, and family, criminal, and civil law. The religion of Islam encompasses three basic elements—*aqidah*, *akhlaq*, and *Shari'a* , which are the roots of Islamic banking and finance.

Aqidah is an Islamic term meaning "a creed" and, by definition, excludes any supposition, doubt, or suspicion on the part of the believer (Al-Qari, no date). It concerns all aspects of the faith and beliefs of a Muslim.

Akhlaq defines the Islamic ethical code and says how it relates to a Muslim's personal conduct. The term is derived from the Arabic *khuluq*, which aligns a person's character with his or her personal qualities and morals. *Akhlaq* includes the commands and prohibitions that govern a Muslim's personal and professional behavior, attitude, transactions, and work ethic.

Figure 2.1. Overview of Islam

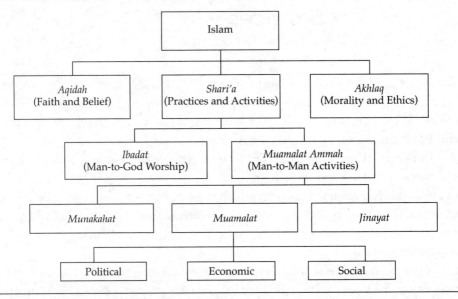

Source: Bank Islam Malaysia (1994).

Figure 2.2. Major and Minor Sources of *Shari'a*

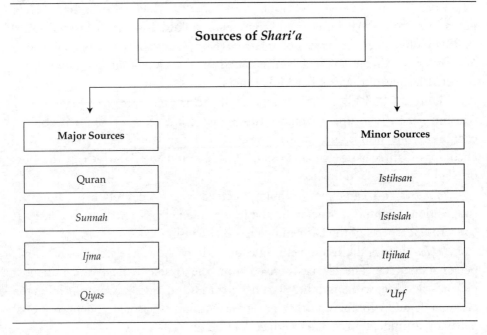

Shari'a, defined previously, is the law of Allah and concerns all aspects (material and spiritual) of a Muslim's life and actions. Its basic values are permanent and universal and are not confined to a specific place or time. According to the teachings of Islam, *Shari'a* protects and promotes religion, life, progeny or family, the intellect, and property or wealth (Abdullah 2005). The Islamic banking system is linked to *Shari'a* through the concept of *muamalat*, which encompasses a broad range of activities—political, economic, and social. *Muamalat* is concerned with the human-to-human relationship, in contrast to the human-to-God relationship known as *ibadat*. *Muamalat* addresses the practicalities of a Muslim's daily life, including the Muslim's relationship with not only other humans but also with animals, plants, and nonliving things.

Shari'a: Islamic Law

Shari'a rulings categorize the nature of a person's actions—namely, whether the action is obligatory, recommended, permissible, reprehensible, or prohibited—as follows:

- *Wajib* is an obligatory act. Performing an act that is *wajib* leads to reward from Allah; failing to perform the act, such as prayer, attracts a penalty in this world and in the hereafter. For the Islamic faithful to practice their religion is obligatory.
- *Sunnat/mandub* is a commendable act, one that is recommended but not binding. A Muslim will be rewarded by Allah for performing an act that is *sunnat*, such as extra prayers and charitable acts, but will not be penalized for failing to perform it.
- *Mubah/harus* is a permissible act, one about which *Shari'a* is neutral. Acting or not acting upon something *mubah*, such as eating, attracts no reward or penalty.
- *Makruh* is an act that is discouraged but not explicitly forbidden. No reward or penalty is associated with performing a *makruh* act, such as divorce.
- *Haram* is a forbidden activity and is considered a major sin. A *haram* activity is punishable by Allah, and avoidance of *haram* activities, such as gambling and drinking, is rewarded.

Sources of *Shari'a*

Muslims believe that Islamic law was revealed by Allah to the Prophet Muhammad. The law consists of a set of rules dealing with how Muslims should conduct their lives in this world. Figure 2.2 lists the major and minor sources of Islamic law.

First, the Quran is regarded by followers of Islam as the immutable and final revelation of Allah. It is considered to be both divine and eternal because it represents the true words of Allah (Al-Omar and Abdel-Haq 1996). Muslims believe that it is the only book of God that has not been distorted and that it awakens in humans the higher consciousness of their relationship with Allah and the universe. The Quran serves as guidance for Muslims' success in both the material and spiritual realms of their lives.

The Quran is the primary source of Islamic law. It provides not only directives relating to personal conduct but also principles relating to all aspects of the economic, social, and cultural lives of Muslims. The Quran consists of 114 chapters, of unequal lengths, called *sura* (the singular form is *surat*), which literally means "eminence" or "high degree." The chapters are divided into verses called *ayah* (the singular form is *ayat*), which means "sign" or "communication from Allah."

The Quran is the principal guidance for structuring Islamic banking products and services. It contains a number of divine injunctions forbidding *riba* (charged interest) and the inappropriate consumption of wealth. It also advocates that commercial engagements be conducted through written contracts.

Second, *Sunnah* is believed by Muslims to be the authentic sayings and reported actions of the Prophet Muhammad (whereas the Quran is considered to be the actual words of Allah). *Sunnah* is Arabic for "method" and explains the instructions of the Quran by making certain implicit Quranic injunctions explicit by providing essential elements and details to facilitate their practice. The three kinds of *Sunnah* are as follows (Nyazee 2002):

- *qual*, or a saying of the Prophet Muhammad that has a bearing on a religious question,
- *fi'l*, an action or practice of the Prophet, and
- *taqrir*, or silent approval of the Prophet of the action or practice of another.

Third, *ijma* is derived from the Arabic *ajma'a*, which means "to determine" and "to agree upon something." It originally referred to the infallible consensus of qualified legal scholars in a certain time period over a particular religious matter. *Ijma* is needed to address the practical problems in the implementation of *Shari'a*, and today, it denotes the consensus of scholars and the importance of delegated legislation to the Muslim community. It is considered sufficient evidence for legal action because, as stated in the *Sunnah*, the Prophet Muhammad said, "My community will never agree in error" (Enayat 2005, p. 20). Thus, the agreement of the scholars of Islam on any religious matter is a source of law in Islam (Kamali 2005).

Fourth, *qiyas* is a method that uses analogy (comparison) to derive Islamic legal rulings for new worldly developments. Qualified legal scholars use *qiyas*, or preceding rulings (precedents), to derive a new ruling for situations that are not addressed by the Quran or the *Sunnah*. Essentially, *qiyas* is the process of taking an established ruling from Islamic law and applying it to a new case that shares the same basic elements addressed by the original ruling. Scholars have developed detailed principles of *qiyas* in the books of Islamic jurisprudence.

The four minor sources of *Shari'a* are the *istihsan*, *istislah*, *itjihad*, and *'urf.*

Istihsan is the use of personal interpretation to avoid the rigidity and unfairness that might result from the literal application of Islamic law. *Istihsan* is an Arabic word that means "to deem something preferable." Based on *istihsan* and a consensus among Islamic jurists, certain forms of contracts that do not conform to the accepted principles of *Shari'a* are permitted. Some legal experts consider the concept of *istihsan* to be similar to the concept of equity in Western law. *Istihsan* plays a prominent role in adapting Islamic law to the changing needs of society.

Istislah is a method used by Muslim jurists to solve perplexing problems that have no clear answers in sacred religious texts. It is related to the Arabic *maslahat*, which can be interpreted as being "in the public interest." The Islamic scholar Abu Hamid Muhammad ibn Muhammad al-Ghazali describes *maslahat* as that which secures a benefit, or prevents harm, and it is associated with the protection of life, religion, intellect, lineage, and property. Any measure that secures these five essential values falls within the scope of *maslahat*. *Maslahat* applies only if it is in compliance with *Shari'a* (Tamadontas 2002).

Itjihad literally means "striving" or "self-exertion." It is the concept that allows Islamic law to adapt to situations or issues not addressed in the Quran or the *Sunnah* (or *hadith*, the oral traditions relating to the words and deeds of Muhammad). The propriety or justification of *itjihad* is measured by its harmony with the Quran and the *Sunnah* (Khir et al. 2007).

'Urf, or custom, can be defined as recurring practices that are acceptable to people of sound nature. It is accepted as a basis for rulings and judgments as long as it does not contravene or contradict Islamic values and principles. Islamic jurists have described *'urf* as the words and deeds acceptable to the citizens of a given region (Shakur 2001). It is based on the principle that "what is proven by custom is alike that proven by *Shari'a*" if that custom is not in conflict with the rules, essence, and spirit of *Shari'a* (Khir et al. 2007, p. 23). *'Urf* is essentially local or regional practice, whereas *ijma* is based on the agreement of the community of legal scholars of Islam and *Shari'a* across regions and countries.

Islamic Contract Law

Islamic banking operates under Islamic commercial law, or *fiqh-al-muamalat*, which deals with contracts and the legal ramifications of contracts. Contracts may be categorized as valid, invalid, or void. The contract is the basis of Islamic business and is the measure of a transaction's validity. A contract also means an engagement or agreement between two persons in a legally accepted, meaningful, and binding manner.

Aqad is the Arabic term for contract and means a tie or a knot that binds two parties together. The word *aqad* is also used in the sense of confirming an oath. In legal terminology, *aqad* refers to a contract between two parties on a particular matter, which is to be concluded upon the offer and the acceptance of the parties concerned (Billah 2006).

The various forms of commercial contracts in Islam can be identified in the Quran and in the jurisprudence of ancient and modern Islamic scholars.

Essential Elements of a Valid Islamic Contract. Islamic banking deals with many types of contracts and other documentation related to deposit, financing, and investment products. Certain conditions must be met for an Islamic contract to be valid. The contract must include the following essential elements to ensure transparency and, if adopted in the true spirit of the elements, to reduce the potential for disputes:

- Offerer and offeree: A contract cannot be formed in the presence of a single party. Although a single person's intent may lead to a number of self-imposed obligations, such as remitting a debt or declaring a charitable donation, these commitments are not considered to be a contract according to *Shari'a*.
- Offer and acceptance: A contract must have an offer (*ijab*) and an acceptance (*qabul*), and both must be executed at the same time. Either party to the contract—buyer or seller—may make an offer. The offer and acceptance may be oral or in writing and may be made by signs or gestures or executed through an agent. A contract is binding upon acceptance regardless of whether it is written or oral.
- Subject matter and consideration: The subject matter and consideration must be lawful under *Shari'a* and must not involve materials or acts that are not *Shari'a* compliant. They should also exist at the time the contract is made and be deliverable. In addition, the quality, quantity, and specifications of the subject matter should be known to both parties. The price, or consideration, must be determined when the contract is made.

In addition, the parties to an Islamic contract must be legally knowledgeable (Bakar 2005) and should not be a minor, insolvent, prodigal, intoxicated, or of unsound mind. No party to the contract should be under any kind of duress or force. If any of the preceding situations apply, the contract will be null and void.

Classification of Islamic Contracts. Contracts in *Shari'a* can be classified in a variety of ways, as listed in **Figure 2.3**. The following three contract classifications are said to be based on "nature" (that is, on an offer, an acceptance, and some consideration, which are regarded as validating a contract in most cultures):

- A *unilateral* contract is a contract written entirely by one party (the offerer) with the second party (the offeree) having only the option to accept or reject the terms of the contract. The contract is binding upon the offerer, is conditional on performance by the offeree, and stipulates compensation for the accomplishment of a specified task. (This type of binding promise in Islamic law is called *wa'd*. An example of a unilateral contract under Islamic law is the contract offered by a real estate agent to find a house for the offerer. The real estate agent's commission for doing so is stipulated in the contract. When the agent finds a house that meets the parameters outlined in the contract, he or she is entitled to the commission. Other examples of unilateral contracts are gifts, wills, and endowments.

Figure 2.3. Classifications of *Shari'a* Contracts

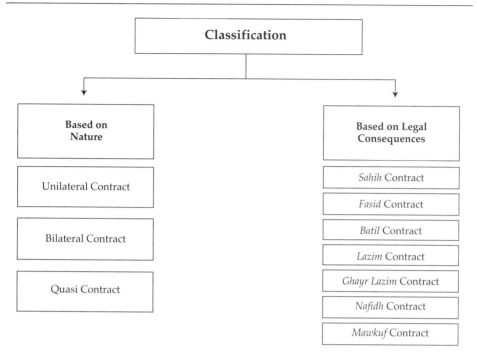

Sources: Billah (2006) and Nyazee (2002).

- A *bilateral* contract is a promise made by one party in exchange for the performance of a stated act by another, and both parties are bound by their exchange of promises. It includes contracts of exchange, partnership, and usufruct (the legal right to use and derive profit or benefit from property belonging to another person or entity). The contract comes into existence the moment the promises of the offerer and offeree are exchanged. A common example of a bilateral contract under Islamic law is the agreement of two parties on the sale/purchase of a car. One party consents to sell the car to a second party who consents to buy the car with an obligation to pay the agreed-upon consideration.
- A *quasi contract* is not considered a true contract under Islamic law, but the agreement of the parties gives rise to an obligation similar to that of a contract. In a quasi contract, the terms are accepted and followed as if a legitimate contract exists. Many casual employment arrangements are quasi contracts because, although a formal contractual arrangement is absent, a contract is "apparently present" and accepted by the parties.

Seven classifications of contracts are based on legal consequences—that is, on compliance with the essential requirements and conditions of the contract.

- A *sahih* contract (valid contract) is one that contains no element prohibited under *Shari'a*. The contract is enforceable and creates an obligation and legal liability for the contracting parties. Three conditions must be met in a *sahih* contract (Nyazee 2002): (1) All the elements required by law must be complete; (2) the additional conditions must be fulfilled; (3) the purpose of the contract and its subject matter must be legal and in compliance with *Shari'a*.
- A *fasid* contract (invalid contract) fulfills all the essential conditions of a *sahih* contract, but because of an irregularity, it lacks validity. The irregularity could be a forbidden term in the contract or an external attribute attached to the contract that is prohibited by Islamic lawmakers. Examples include a contract signed under coercion and a sale contract for which the object of sale does not exist.
- A *batil* contract (void contract) is void because its elements and conditions are not in compliance with *Shari'a*. Such a contract has no legal effects and is invalid and unenforceable (Khir et al. 2007). Ownership is not transferable, nor is any other obligation of performance created in a *batil* contract. Examples are contracts to sell liquor and those signed by a minor.
- A *lazim* contract is binding and irrevocable, retrospectively and prospectively, for both parties. Neither party has the right to terminate the contract without the consent of the other unless the option to revoke the contract has been granted beforehand (Nyazee 2002). Examples are sales and lease contracts.
- A *ghayr lazim* (or *jaiz*) contract provides that either party may unilaterally terminate it at any time on the basis of the conditions specified in the contract. Examples of such nonbinding contracts are agencies and partnerships.
- A *nafidh* contract is an immediate agreement that does not involve a third party.
- A *mawkuf* contract is a valid but suspended contract. Examples include a contract that lacks proper authority and a contract in which one party suffers from a terminal illness.

Contracts in Islamic Banking

In Islamic banking, contracts play an important role in ensuring transparency and structuring transactions so that conformity with Islamic law is maintained. In Islamic law, rules are prescribed for specific contracts as illustrated in **Figure 2.4.**

Contract of Exchange. The sales contract (*bai* contract) is the primary contract of exchange in Islamic commercial law. It involves the transfer of ownership

Figure 2.4. Key Types of Islamic Contracts in Islamic Banking

Contract of Exchange	Contract of Usufruct	Gratuitous Contract	Participation Contract	Supporting Contract
Murabahah	*Ijarah*	*Hibah*	*Mudharabah*	*Kafalah*
Bai' Bithaman Ajil	*Al-Ijarah Thumma Al-Bai*	*Qard*	*Musaqat*	*Rahnu*
Bai' Salam	*Ijarah Muntahia Bittamleek*	*Ibra*	*Musyarakah*	*Hiwalah*
Bai' Istisna				*Wakalah*
Bai' Istijrar				*Wadiah*
Bai' Inah				*Jualah*

Source: Adawiah (2007).

of a lawful commodity for a fixed price or for another commodity (barter trade). Sales contracts are used extensively in Islamic banking and include the following:

- *Murabahah* contract (cost-plus-markup contract) involves the sale of lawful goods at a price that includes an agreed-upon profit margin for the bank (seller). It is mandatory for the bank to declare to the customer the cost and profit. Payment can be, depending on the agreement between the parties, spot or deferred.

- *Bai' bithaman ajil* contract (deferred-payment sale) is a sale of goods on a deferred-payment basis. The bank purchases an asset and sells it to the customer at cost plus a profit margin agreed to by both parties. The bank is not required to disclose the price and profit margin. Payments can be monthly, quarterly, or semiannually.

- *Bai' salam* contract (forward contract) refers to an agreement whereby payment is made in advance for delivery of specified goods in the future. The underlying asset does not exist at the time of the sale. This type of contract is used in agricultural financing. Funds are advanced to farmers who deliver their harvested crops to the bank to sell in the market.

- *Bai' istisna* contract (supplier contract) is an agreement in which the price of an asset is paid in advance but the asset is manufactured or otherwise produced and delivered at a later date. This type of contract is typically used in the manufacturing and construction sectors.

- *Bai' istijrar* contract (also a type of supplier contract) refers to an agreement between a purchaser and a supplier whereby the supplier agrees to deliver a specified product on a periodic schedule at an agreed-upon price rather than an agreed-upon mode of payment by the purchaser.

- *Bai' inah* contract (sale and buyback contract) involves the sale and buyback of an asset. The seller sells the asset on a cash basis, but the purchaser buys back the asset at a price higher than the cash price on a deferred basis. This type of contract is primarily used in Malaysia for cash financing; it is also used for Islamic credit cards.

Contract of Usufruct. Usufruct contracts govern the legal right to use and profit or benefit from property that belongs to another person. The key usufruct contracts in practice in Islamic banking are the following:

- *Ijarah* (leasing) refers to an arrangement in which a bank (the lessor) leases equipment, a building, or other facilities to a client (the lessee) at an agreed-upon rental fee and for a specified duration. Ownership of the equipment remains in the hands of the lessor.
- *Al-ijarah thumma al-bai* (leasing and subsequent purchase) is a type of *ijarah* contract in combination with a *bai* (purchase) contract. Under the terms of the *ijarah* (leasing) contract, the lessee leases the goods from the owner, or lessor, at an agreed-upon rental fee for a specified period of time. Upon expiry of the leasing period, the lessee enters into the *bai* contract to purchase the goods from the lessor at an agreed-upon price. This concept is similar to a hire/purchase contract or closed-end leasing as practiced by conventional banks.
- *Ijarah muntahia bittamleek* (buyback leasing) involves an *ijarah* (leasing) contract that includes a guarantee by the lessor to transfer the ownership in the leased property to the lessee, either at the end of the term of the *ijarah* period or by stages during the term of the contract.

Gratuitous Contracts. A gratuitous contract is entered into for a benevolent purpose, such as for making a charitable donation. The following are the gratuitous contracts currently used by Islamic banks:

- *Hibah* refers to a gift awarded by a bank without any commensurate exchange. For example, a bank gives *hibah* to a savings account holder as a token of appreciation for keeping money in the account.
- *Qard* involves an interest-free loan that is extended as good will or on a benevolent basis. The borrower is required to repay only the principal amount of the loan. The borrower may choose to pay an extra amount, however, as a token of appreciation for the lender. No extra payment over the principal amount can be charged by the bank; any such extra charge is considered *riba* (charged interest), which is prohibited under Islamic law. These loans are intended for individual clients in financial distress.
- *Ibra* occurs when a bank withdraws its right to collect payment from a borrower. The computation of *ibra*, a rebate, is based on the terms and conditions set forth in the governing contract.

Participation Contracts. *Shari'a*, in order to promote risk-and-reward sharing consistent with the principles of Islam, encourages wealth creation from partnership arrangements that are governed by the following types of participation contracts:

- *Mudharabah* (trust financing) is a partnership between a bank and a customer in which the bank provides the capital for a project and the customer or entrepreneur uses his or her expertise to manage the investment. Profits arising from the investment are shared between the bank and the entrepreneur on the basis of an agreed-upon profit-sharing ratio. If the project results in a loss, it is borne solely by the bank.

- *Musyarakah* (partnership financing) refers to an investment partnership in which all partners share in a project's profits on the basis of a specified ratio but losses are shared in proportion to the amount of capital invested. All parties to the contract are entitled to participate in the management of the investment, but they are not required to do so. A *musyarakah mutanaqisah* (diminishing partnership) is an agreement in which the customer (the partner of the bank) eventually becomes the complete and sole owner of the investment for which the bank has provided the funds. The profits generated by the investment are distributed to the bank on the basis of its share of the profits and also a predetermined portion of the customer's profits. The payment of this portion of the customer's share of profits results in reducing the bank's ownership in the investment.

- *Musaqat*, a form of *musyarakah*, refers to an arrangement between a farmer, or garden owner, and a worker who agrees to water the garden and perform other chores in support of a bountiful harvest. The harvest is shared among all parties according to their respective contributions.

Supporting Contracts. The supporting contracts used in Islamic banking include the following:

- *Kafalah* contract (guaranteed contract) refers to a contract in which the contracting party or any third party guarantees the performance of the contract terms by the contracting party.

- *Rahnu* (collateralized financing) is an arrangement whereby a valuable asset is placed as collateral for payment of an obligation. If the debtor fails to make the payments specified in the contract, the creditor can dispose of the asset to settle the debt. Any surplus after the settlement of the sale is returned to the owner of the asset.

- *Hiwalah* (remittance) involves a transfer of funds/debt from the depositor's/debtor's account to the receiver's/creditor's account; a commission may be charged for the service. This contract is used for settling international accounts by book transfers. It obviates, to a large extent, the necessity of a physical transfer of cash. Examples are a bill of exchange and a promissory note.

- *Wakalah* (nominating another person to act) deals with a situation in which a representative is appointed to undertake transactions on another person's behalf, usually for a fee.
- *Wadiah* contract (safekeeping contract) refers to a deposit of goods or funds with a person who is not the owner for safekeeping purposes. This type of contract is used for savings and current accounts in Islamic banks. Because *wadiah* is a trust, the depository institution (bank) becomes the guarantor of the funds, thus guaranteeing repayment of the entire amount of the deposit, or any part of it outstanding in the account of depositors, when demanded. The depositors are not entitled to any share of the profits earned on the funds deposited with the bank, but the bank may provide *hibah* (a monetary gift) to the depositors as a token of appreciation for keeping the money with the bank.
- *Jualah* contract (a unilateral contract for a task) is an agreement in which a reward, such as a wage or a stipend, is promised for the accomplishment of a specified task or service. In Islamic banking, this type of contract applies to bank charges and commissions for services rendered by the bank.

Summary

Shari'a provides the foundation for modern *Shari'a*-compliant economic and financial transactions. Thus, *Shari'a* supplies the philosophy and principles underpinning Islamic banking products and services. Islamic banking, based on Islamic law, is an integral part of the attempt to develop the Islamic ideal in social and economic terms.

In this chapter, we reviewed the sources of *Shari'a*, the types of Islamic contracts, and the specific contracts used in Islamic banking. The Islamic legal system possesses a certain flexibility that provides for adaptation to new socio-economic situations in that Islamic law deals differently with permanent aspects of legal issues and changeable aspects of legal issues. Islamic law allows room for reasoning and reinterpretation in areas of law that are changeable and progressive in character. For example, *riba* (interest) is a fixed prohibition whereas the ruling of permissibility for *gharar* (uncertainty) takes into account a cost–benefit analysis. Hence, permissibility changes with changing technology, the legal framework, customary practice, and so forth (see, for example, Bakar 2005).

Chapter 3. Islamic Banking: Sources and Uses of Funds

Once regarded as a specialized backwater of global banking, Islamic banking has gained substantial strength in the world of international finance. It is developing into a full-fledged financial system offering a broad range of *Shari'a*-compliant products and services to meet the needs of individuals and institutions. At year-end 2007, global Islamic banking assets totaled approximately US$500 billion, a growth rate of nearly 30 percent in 2007 alone (Eaves 2008). And according to Standard & Poor's, over the last decade, *Shari'a*-compliant financial assets have grown at a 10 percent annual clip (Robinson 2007). In September 2008, Morgan Stanley forecasted that *Shari'a*-compliant banking deposit assets would reach US$1 trillion in 2010 ("Morgan Stanley Says . . ." 2008).

Since its inception in the early 1960s, modern Islamic banking has been widely adopted throughout the Muslim world. In this period, Islamic finance has expanded in complexity through the creation of new *Shari'a*-compliant products in response to the increasing global demand for such products. Viewed by many as a financing system that encourages entrepreneurship, Islamic banking and finance are making inroads into the areas of commercial and investment banking.

This chapter focuses on how Islamic financial products are structured and explains the mechanics of Islamic banking, which operates without charging interest on borrowed funds.

Islamic Banking Overview

Unlike conventional banks, Islamic banks are not allowed to charge interest by lending money to their customers because, under Islamic commercial law, making money from money (*riba*) is strictly prohibited. In Islamic finance, money is not considered a commodity and, therefore, cannot be "rented out" for a fee. In lieu of charging interest on money lent, Islamic banking practices and financial transactions are based primarily on sharing (for instance, *musharka*), trading (for example, *murabahah*), or leasing (*ijarah*). The contracts for profit-and-loss sharing are preferred from a *Shari'a* perspective, although in practice, industry relies on trading or leasing, in which the bank sells an asset to the customer on an installment basis or leases the asset to the customer and earns a fixed return in that way.

In contrast, conventional banks charge interest on loans made to customers and pay interest on customers' deposits. The bank charges a higher rate of interest on loans made than it pays on deposits and thus earns a profit from the spread between the interest rate on its assets (the rate on the loans it makes) and the rate on its liabilities (the rate it pays depositors).

Another difference between Islamic and conventional banking is that Islamic banks do not follow the principle of having a fractional reserve requirement. Conventional banks operate with a fractional reserve requirement that is applied to transaction accounts (commonly referred to as checking accounts). Savings accounts and time deposits are not subject to a reserve requirement.

In a fractional reserve system, a bank can loan funds equal to the reciprocal of the reserve requirement. For example, a 10 percent reserve requirement on a deposit of $100 allows the bank to loan up to $90 while maintaining the other $10 of the $100 deposit to meet normal withdrawal requests. If the full $90 is loaned out and deposited in another bank, that bank, which is also subject to the 10 percent reserve requirement, can then make new loans of $81. The process continues until the initial deposit of $100 has been multiplied 10 times to $1,000. The rationale behind a fractional reserve banking system is that under normal circumstances, only a portion of a bank's deposits will be needed to meet customer redemptions. The central bank acts as a lender of last resort if a bank is unable to replenish a low reserve position by borrowing in the money markets, selling assets, or drawing on lines of credit.

Fractional reserve banking is not *Shari'a* compliant because it is accomplished through the creation of loans on which interest is charged. This interest is strictly prohibited under Islamic banking.

Islamic finance comprises features of both commercial and investment banking. **Figure 3.1** outlines the general approach to profit generation for an Islamic bank, beginning with the sources of funds. The figure shows that Islamic banks make a profit by mobilizing the savings of investors to meet the financial requirements of borrowers. The sources of funds of an Islamic bank include deposits in various accounts and deposits in special investment accounts that are earmarked for borrowing by corporate investors to fund specific projects. Shareholder funds are also a source of funds for Islamic banks. All of these sources of funds are channeled into general financing, trade financing (working capital, domestic and international import- and export-related financing, and so forth), country treasury products (Islamic money market instruments), and other services.

An Islamic bank shares in the profit and loss of each borrower's business transaction. In turn, the bank divides its share of profits and losses with its general and special investors who have deposited funds in the bank. Profit is calculated *ex post* and is determined by the outcome of the borrowers' business transactions. The profit earned by a bank is reduced by the bank's operating expenses, by *zakat* (the Islamic welfare tax), and by government taxes before it is shared with shareholders as dividends (Shanmugam and Gupta 2007).

Sources of Funds. Islamic banks are deposit-taking institutions but do not pay interest on deposits. Their sources of funds include shareholder investments, savings accounts, current accounts, and investment accounts, classified as either

Figure 3.1. Overview of Profit Mechanism in Islamic Banking

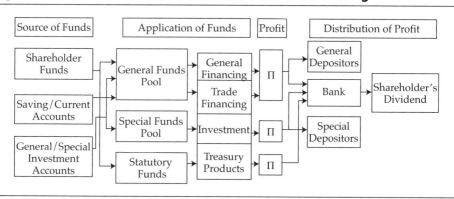

Source: "Islamic Banks Are on the Rise" (2008).

general or special. Similar to conventional bank depositors, Islamic banking depositors are seeking safe custody of their funds and convenience in using their funds. Islamic banking depositors may also expect to earn some profit on deposit balances, but this profit is not guaranteed. Account holders may use automated teller machine (ATM) facilities, internet and mobile banking, and international debit cards.

 ▓ *Shareholder funds.* An Islamic bank may raise initial equity by following the principle of *musyarakah* (equity participation). Under this principle, the capital owner enters into a partnership with the bank by contributing equity in return for a share of the bank's profit or loss on the basis of a predetermined ratio (for example, 70 percent/30 percent or 60 percent/40 percent), with the larger fraction due the investor.

 ▓ Wadiah *savings accounts.* Islamic banks practice the principle of *wadiah* in operating customer savings accounts. The structure of the *wadiah* savings account offering is illustrated in **Figure 3.2**. The bank may request permission to use customer funds deposited in these accounts as long as these funds will remain within the bank's discretion. The bank does not share with the customer profits earned from the use of the customer's funds but does guarantee the customer's deposits. The bank may, however, reward customers with a *hibah* (gift) as a token of its appreciation for being allowed to use the funds. *Hibah* could be a portion of the profit generated from the use of the funds. *Hibah* may be paid at any time, but in practice, most Islamic banks pay *hibah* at a regular periodic interval, such as quarterly or semiannually.

 ▓ *Current accounts.* The current account is a deposit account that can be used for business or personal purposes and, like a savings account, is based on the Islamic principle of *wadiah*. Account holders are not guaranteed any return for keeping their funds with the bank, but they may be rewarded with *hibah*. Customer current account balances are guaranteed. The primary distinction between savings and current accounts is that minimum balance limits and withdrawals are more flexible for current accounts.

Figure 3.2. Structure of *Wadiah* Savings Account

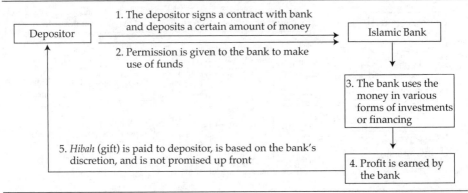

In certain countries, such as Iran, the principle of *qard hassan* (a benevolent or interest-free loan) governs the use of depositors' funds by the bank. In this case, deposits are treated as benevolent loans by the depositor to the bank, so the bank is free to use the funds in a *qard hassan* current account without permission of the depositor. The depositor (in the role of lender) is not entitled to any return on the use of the funds, which would constitute *riba*. As in the *wadiah* savings account, the bank guarantees that the amount deposited will be returned.

■ *Investment accounts*. Investment accounts operate on the principle of *mudharabah* (profit sharing), with banks accepting deposits from investors for either a fixed or unlimited period of time. Investment accounts are also known as "profit-and-loss–sharing" deposits. The ratio for sharing profits and losses identifies the only return guarantee the account holder receives from the bank.

For this kind of arrangement, the customer is referred to as an "investor" (*rabb-ul-mal*) with the characteristics of a silent partner. The bank acts as an agent (*mudarib*) for the investor in the management of the funds and invests them in *Shari'a*-compliant stocks, economic projects, and so forth. Although these accounts are known as profit-and-loss–sharing accounts, all investment losses are borne solely by the investor, except when the loss results from the bank's misconduct or negligence. In general, Islamic banks do not charge any investment management fee; the returns are mainly from shared profits (Ebrahim and Joo 2001). Investment accounts are an important source of funds for Islamic banks and are used for investment and financing activities. According to Björklund and Lundstrom (2004), Islamic banks seek to earn a profit on investment accounts, in contrast to their expectations for savings or current account deposits, which are more likely to be held for precautionary or transaction purposes to serve the needs of customers. The transaction structure for *mudharabah*-based financial products is illustrated in **Figure 3.3**.

Figure 3.3. Structure of *Mudharabah*-Based Financial Products

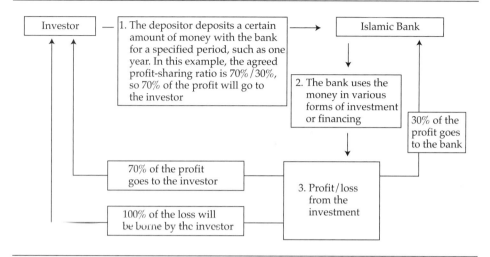

An investment account may be classified as follows:

- *Mudharabah mutlaqah* (general investment account): In this type of account, the investor, or account holder, authorizes the bank to invest the funds in any *Shari'a*-compliant investment manner deemed appropriate by the bank. No restrictions are imposed on the use of the funds.

- *Mudharabah muqayyadah* (special investment account): In this type of account, the investor, or account holder, may impose conditions, restrictions, or preferences regarding where, how, and for what purpose the funds are to be invested. The bank is required to fulfill the investor's requests and ensure that the investments are *Shari'a* compliant.

Recently, banks have chosen to operate savings accounts on the principle of *mudharabah* to provide better returns to account holders and to gain a competitive edge in the market.

Table 3.1 summarizes the main sources of funds for Islamic banks and compares their account features.

Applications of Funds. Recall that the basis of Islamic finance is risk sharing between the parties in an underlying asset-based transaction, so profit-and-loss sharing is a prominent feature of Islamic finance. Recall also that Islamic financial products and practices must avoid *gharar* (uncertainty, risk, and speculation) and pursue investment in *halal* (religiously permissible) activities. Islamic modes of finance fall into the following three broad categories (Al-Jarhi, no date):

- *Equity financing and profit sharing*: In both equity financing and profit-sharing activities, the bank provides funds to an enterprise in return for a share of the profits generated by the borrowed funds. The distinction between the two

Table 3.1. Sources of Funds in Islamic Banking

Account Type	Objective	Principal Value Guaranteed?	Profit-Sharing Method	Risk
Wadiah savings account	Precaution and to earn a profit	Yes	*Hibah* at bank's discretion	None
Wadiah current account	To have liquidity available on demand	Yes	Generally no profit sharing	None
Qard hassan current account	To have liquidity available on demand	Yes	Generally no profit sharing	None
General investment account	To earn a profit	No	Profit sharing at negotiated ratio	High
Special investment account	To earn a profit	No	Profit sharing at negotiated ratio	High

Source: Björklund and Lundstrom (2004).

structures is that equity financing allows the bank to participate in the enterprise's decision making. Profit-sharing arrangements preclude bank participation in the borrower's management decisions.

- *Credit purchases*: For credit purchase transactions, the bank provides immediate delivery of the goods or services sought by the customer in exchange for the customer promising to make a series of deferred payments to the bank equal to the cost of the goods or services plus a markup.
- *Leasing*: In leasing arrangements, the bank purchases a durable asset and leases it to the customer in return for regular payments that reflect the cost of holding and maintaining the asset.

In general, penalties imposed by Islamic banks for late payment or default are not collected for the bank's own benefit but are donated to charity. Some Muslim countries allow banks to charge a penalty to recoup the costs of collecting the missed payment.

Financing Structures. Islamic banks offer a broad spectrum of financial structures, ranging from simple *Shari'a*-compliant retail products, such as savings and current accounts, to leasing, trust financing, and large-scale infrastructure financing. Not all of the financial structures described are acceptable to all Muslim investors. This controversy is a byproduct of the different schools of Islamic thought and their various interpretations. No single body currently serves as the mediator of these differences of opinion. Financing structures include the following.

Bai' bithaman ajil. *Bai' bithaman ajil* (BBA) financing refers to the sale of goods by a bank to a customer on a deferred-payment basis over a specified period at a price that includes a markup or profit margin agreed to by both parties. Deferred payments may be made in monthly installments. A BBA plan is commonly used for financing the purchase of real property, vehicles, or consumer goods and is predominantly a Malaysian practice. The BBA structure is controversial; supporters of the structure argue that the profit earned is justified under *Shari'a* because it is derived from a buy-and-sell transaction and is not considered interest accrued from the lending of money.

BBA financing involves essentially three separate agreements. In the case of real property, the first agreement details the bank's purchase of the property from the developer. In the second agreement, the bank sells the property to the customer. And the third agreement stipulates that the bank can sell the property in the event of default by the customer. **Figure 3.4** depicts such a typical BBA transaction structure.

Figure 3.4. Structure of Fixed-Rate *Bai' Bithaman Ajil* Financing

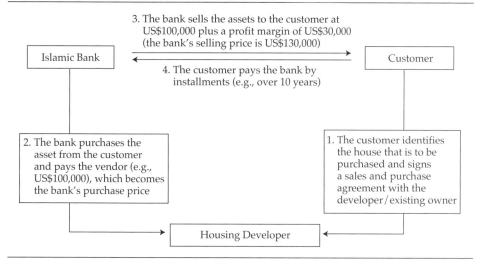

At year-end 2003, according to statistics compiled by Malaysia's central bank, Bank Negara Malaysia, 87.8 percent of total Islamic financing was in fixed-rate instruments, 58.8 percent of which were long term in nature.[6] Therefore, in 2003, Bank Negara Malaysia introduced a variable-rate BBA product to:

> enable the Islamic financial institutions which operate in a dual banking environ-
> ment [Islamic and conventional banking] to . . . match the current market
> financing rate in order to give matching returns to their depositors. . . . ("Intro-
> duction of Islamic Variable Rate Mechanism" no date, p. 1)

---

[6]See "Introduction of Islamic Variable Rate Mechanism" (no date).

In a variable-rate BBA, the contractual selling price and the customer's payment installments are higher than in a fixed-rate BBA, which guarantees the bank a profit (the ceiling profit rate) higher than that of a fixed-rate BBA. A waiver of the right to claim unearned profit is given to the bank by the customer to permit the bank to grant rebates (*ibra*) of the unearned profit to the customer by reducing the contracted monthly installment amount that the customer must pay. This flexibility in determining the monthly installment amount gives the BBA its variable-rate characteristic.

Figure 3.5 explains the mechanics of a variable-rate BBA. The financing is created when the bank purchases the asset for cash and immediately sells the asset to the customer on deferred-payment terms. In this example, the ceiling profit rate is set at 12 percent a year and the selling price of the asset is higher than in the case of a fixed-rate BBA. Both parties to the transaction agree on the amount of the monthly installments—in this case, 2,000 Malaysian ringgits (RM2,000)—and on the repayment period.

Assume that in the first month of the repayment period, the benchmark in the pricing calculation is 10 percent a year. The benchmark is the base lending rate (BLR), or market rate, plus the predetermined profit margin. Although the ceiling profit rate is typically capped at 400 bps above the BLR, the effective profit margin is usually required to be observed at 250 bps above the BLR.

Figure 3.5. Variable-Rate *Bai' Bithaman Ajil* Financing Structure

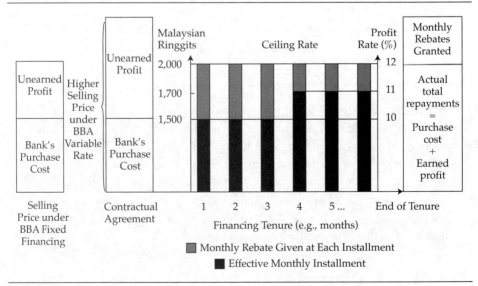

The result is that the bank will give a rebate to the customer in the first month in the amount of RM500. The rebate represents the difference between the ceiling profit rate of 12 percent a year and the effective profit rate of 10 percent a year. If in the fourth month of the repayment period the BLR or market rate rises so that the effective profit rate increases to 11 percent a year, the monthly rebate will be reduced to RM300.

Murabahah. *Murabahah* financing is a popular method used by an Islamic bank to meet the short-term trade-financing needs of its customers. It is often referred to as "cost-plus financing" or "markup financing." In this type of financing, the bank agrees to fund the purchase of a specific asset or goods from a supplier at the request of the customer. Upon acquiring the asset, the bank sells it to the customer at a predetermined markup. **Figure 3.6** illustrates the transaction structure of *murabahah*-based products.

A bank practices *murabahah* financing when it has obtained a legally enforceable promise by the client buyer that he or she will buy the good from the bank once the bank has purchased the good. In this case, because the bank takes constructive or physical receipt of the goods before selling them to its customer, the bank accepts whatever risk is inherent in the transaction, such as the risk that the asset is destroyed while in the bank's possession. Thus, any profit from the transaction is considered to be derived from a service and is legitimate under Islamic law. The customer's repayment schedule may be in equal or staggered installments or in a lump sum. The goods must be in the possession of the bank before being sold to the customer; this aspect is the critical element that allows the transaction to be *Shari'a* compliant (Ahmad 1993).

Figure 3.6. Structure of *Murabahah* Financing

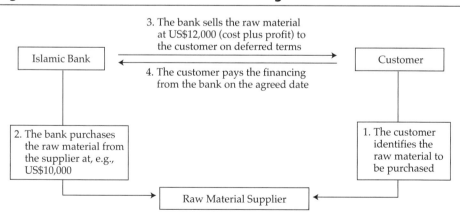

Murabahah financing has become the backbone of contemporary Islamic banking. It is commonly used for financing the purchase of raw materials, machinery, equipment, and consumer durables. The profit margin is mutually agreed between the client and the bank.

Critics argue that the substance of a *murabahah* transaction is no different from that of a conventional loan because the Islamic bank purchases the goods only after it has obtained a promise from the client that he or she will purchase those goods from the bank; the purchase and sale are processed as quickly as possible so that the length of time goods are owned by the bank is minimized; the trade takes place only if credit is involved; the markup is usually benchmarked to prevailing interest rates; and the amount payable to the bank tends to depend on the length of the credit period. Together, all these elements make the substance of *murabahah* trade the same as a conventional loan, which carries credit risk rather than the risk associated with the ownership of an asset or a business enterprise.

The current form of *murabahah* financing—also known as "*murabahah* to the purchase orderer"—is also materially different from classic *murabahah* financing, which took place before there were banks. Sellers carried inventories and assumed ownership risk of the goods being sold, credit was an exception, spot trading was the rule, and unilateral promises to purchase were not systematically used in conjunction with a sales contract.

Ijarah. *Ijarah* financing or leasing is growing in popularity in the Muslim community. In Arabic, the word "*ijarah*" means "to give something on rent." Under an *ijarah* financing arrangement, the bank purchases a tangible asset based on the client's specifications and leases it to the client. The lease duration varies from three months to five years or more, depending on the nature of the asset and the lessee's requirements.

The Islamic lease differs from a conventional hire/purchase in that the ownership of the asset remains with the bank during the lease period. The bank gives the right of use of the asset to the lessee, as well as physical possession of the asset. In return, the lessee makes rental payments based on an agreed schedule. Upon expiration of the lease, the lessee returns the asset to the lessor (the bank).

Ijarah is typically used for high-cost assets with long life spans. The financing structure for *ijarah*-based products is illustrated in **Figure 3.7**. The owner of the asset, or lessor (the bank), bears all the risks associated with ownership, such as asset maintenance, while the user of the asset (lessee) pays a fixed price (rent) for enjoying the benefits of the asset.

Many scholars are critical of a practice whereby the Islamic bank makes the lessee the actual payer of the *takaful* (Islamic insurance) contribution or premium by passing on the premium costs as part of the lease installments to be paid by the lessee (Ayub 2007). The problem is that some of the risks of ownership may be assumed by the bank but the cost of the transfer of these risks is actually borne by the lessee.

Figure 3.7. Structure of *Ijarah* Financing

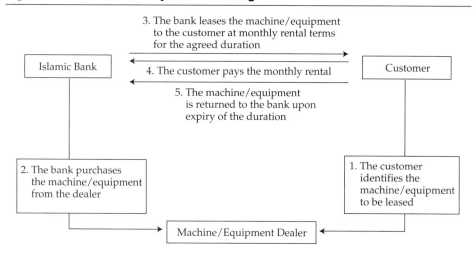

To summarize, an *ijarah* contract is essentially the sale of the usufruct of the asset for a specified period of time. The bank receives profit from the rental of the asset and retains ownership of the asset. The lessee enjoys the immediate benefits of using the asset without incurring a large capital expenditure.

Al-ijarah thumma al-bai. *Al-ijarah thumma al-bai* (AITAB) financing is essentially an *ijarah* (leasing) contract combined with a *bai* (purchase) contract. Under the first contract, the purchaser (customer) leases the goods from the owner (the bank) at an agreed rental price for a specified period. Upon expiration of the leasing period, the purchaser enters into a second contract to purchase the goods from the owner at an agreed price. The transaction can also be referred to as an "*ijarah* contract ending with purchase." The structure for AITAB financing is illustrated in **Figure 3.8**.

As with a straight *ijarah* contract, the bank owns the asset during the leasing period. The purchase agreement (*bai*), which is executed automatically at the end of the leasing period, transfers ownership of the asset to the customer. If the customer fails to carry out the obligation to pay the rental price or otherwise breaches the terms and conditions of the AITAB contract, the bank has the right to exercise reasonable actions to mitigate its losses (Bank Negara Malaysia 2005). The amount of the lease payments is based on the profitability of the asset, not on the bank's capital investment in the asset (Zineldin 1990).

AITAB financing is practiced mainly in Malaysia. Similar products found in the Middle East and other parts of the world are usually based on the principle of *ijarah wa iqtina*—a lease contract with a put and/or call option on the leased asset held by the customer. There is a unilateral undertaking by the bank whereby at the

Figure 3.8. Structure of AITAB Financing

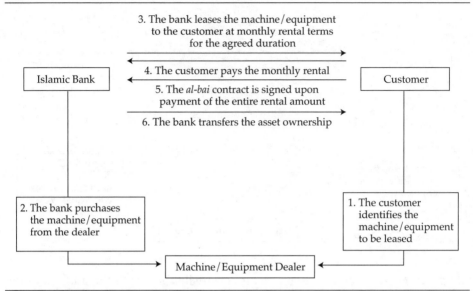

end of the lease period, the ownership of the asset will be transferred to the lessee. The undertaking or the promise given is unilateral and does not become an integral part of the contract. Hence, the undertaking or promise does not become an integral part of the lease contract, whereby it would be conditional.

The rental payments and the purchase price are determined in such a manner that the bank receives its principal invested in the asset plus a profit, or markup.

Musyarakah. *Musyarakah* financing is a type of partnership financing in which one of the partners is an Islamic bank. Profits and losses are shared among the partners according to a predetermined formula. Profit sharing need not be based on the proportion of shares owned, but liability is limited to the contributions of the shareholders. In other words, investors cannot be held liable for more than the amount of capital they invest in the partnership (Shanmugam and Gupta 2007).

The structure of *musyarakah* financing is illustrated in **Figure 3.9**. The partners are entitled to participate in the management and audit operations of the venture, but it is not mandatory that they do so. In addition, the partners are allowed to charge a fee for any managerial efforts or other forms of labor they contribute to the project. The bank may act as a passive (silent) partner while the customer manages the venture. In practice, most banks closely monitor the venture to ensure that it is well managed.

A *musyarakah* partnership or joint venture is often regarded as the purest form of Islamic finance. Only selected banks offer it, however, because many banks consider it highly risky.

Figure 3.9. Structure of *Musyarakah* Financing

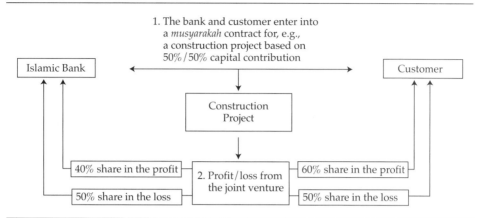

Diminishing *musyarakah* financing is a special form of partnership that culminates in the bank's client owning the asset or project being financed. One partner (the client) promises to gradually buy the shares of the other partner (the bank) until ownership of the asset is completely transferred to the client. This type of financing is widely used in Malaysia to finance the purchase of homes and involves the use of two written contracts, an *ijarah* agreement and a *musyarakah*-diminishing-ownership agreement.[7]

In a *musyarakah*-diminishing-ownership agreement, the bank purchases the house and leases it to the customer on the basis of *ijarah*. Concurrent with the rental payments during the term of the lease, the customer also pays installments to the bank to buy the bank's ownership stake in the property. The bank's ownership stake is divided into a specified number of units, which the client agrees to purchase gradually within a specified time period. Each installment reduces the bank's ownership share in the property. At the end of the financing term, the title of the property passes to the customer.

Istisna. *Istisna* financing involves a contract of exchange providing for deferred delivery of the good or the asset that is being financed. In *istisna* financing, a commodity is purchased or sold before it comes into existence, which is an exception to the *Shari'a* principle requiring that an underlying asset be present in order for a financial transaction to take place. The fact that nothing is exchanged on the spot or at the time of contracting is the unique feature of an *istisna* contract. Both parties agree on the price of the good or asset. The bank purchases the good or asset for sale to the customer on deferred-payment terms.

---

[7]See Meezan Bank (2008).

Istisna financing is most often used to finance construction, shipbuilding, manufacturing projects, or turnkey infrastructure projects. The *istisna* agreement provides flexibility by permitting a transaction to be structured with payment made in advance and delivery of the good or asset at a future date or with both payment and delivery made at a future date.

Commodity *murabahah*. A commodity *murabahah* contract replicates short-term money market deposits for fixed terms of one week to one year. The underlying asset in this structure is a commodity, such as copper, aluminum, lead, palm oil, or crude oil. The structure works as follows. A bank buys the commodity at the spot price, or current price, and sells the commodity to another bank on a deferred-payment basis, perhaps for three months, at the spot price plus a markup (profit). The bank that buys the commodity on a deferred basis immediately sells it to a broker or another institution at the spot price. The first bank makes a profit from the markup in the transaction, and the second bank raises funds it can use immediately for investment.

This financing structure is considered *Shari'a* compliant because the bank's markup is considered profit rather than interest. The portfolio does not include tangible assets; rather, it comprises cash or receivable debts, neither of which are negotiable.

Many scholars criticize commodity *murabahah* financing because it involves trading of commodities that are not needed for use by either party to the contract and because the underlying objective is to lend/borrow money at interest. Nevertheless, it is widely practiced by Islamic banks in many locations.

Tawarruq. Islamic banks use the *tawarruq* structure to facilitate cash financing to their clients. *Tawarruq* financing structure is illustrated in **Figure 3.10**. In this structure, the bank directly or indirectly buys an asset and immediately sells it to a customer on a deferred-payment basis. The customer then sells the same asset to a third party for immediate delivery and payment. The result is that the customer receives an immediate cash payment with an obligation to make deferred payments to the bank for the marked-up price of the asset.

The asset financed is typically a freely tradable commodity, such as platinum or copper. Gold and silver are treated by the *Shari'a* as currency and cannot be used. In modern Islamic banking, the bank usually performs all the transactions needed for *tawarruq* financing.

Tawarruq financing is somewhat controversial and has been the subject of debate in Islamic financial circles because the customer involved has no real intention of buying or selling the underlying commodity that supports the financial transaction. Because of the absence of any exchange of actual goods, *tawarruq* financing is prohibited by the Islamic Fiqh Academy of Jeddah, Saudi Arabia. *Tawarruq* generates debts, adding to the gap between the real sector and the financial sector of the

Figure 3.10. Structure of *Tawarruq* Financing

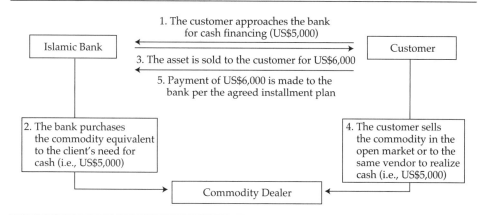

economy. It leads to a debt market, and a debt instrument does not represent any real asset. The customer's purpose when engaging in the transaction is merely to generate cash, which can be construed as inconsistent with *Shari'a*. Mohammad Nejatullah Siddiqi, a prominent researcher in Islamic finance, has said:

> The introduction of *tawarruq* into the body of Islamic economy is sure to act like a virus destroying the immune system that would protect it from increasing indebtedness leading to speculation, monetary fluctuations, instability and inequity. (Siddiqi 2007, p. 4)

Bai' inah. *Bai' inah* financing is a sale-and-buyback transaction that involves two back-to-back *aqad* (agreements). The structure is designed to provide the customer with a cash sum. The bank sells an item to the customer at an agreed price (first agreement) and then buys it back from the customer at a lower price (second agreement). The difference is the bank's profit on the transaction and is predetermined. **Figure 3.11** depicts the structure of *bai' inah* financing.

Bai' inah financing is very similar to *tawarruq* financing, but it is practiced mainly in Malaysia. And like *tawarruq* financing, the *bai' inah* product is somewhat controversial because of its abstract or intangible nature.

Mudharabah. *Mudharabah* financing, which is also known as "trust financing," is based on the *mudharabah* principle of profit sharing. *Mudharabah* financing is a commercial activity in which an Islamic bank entrusts funds to an entrepreneur. The arrangement enables the entrepreneur to carry out business projects. Profits are distributed between the bank and the entrepreneur on the basis of a predetermined ratio. All losses are borne by the supplier of the funds (the bank) as long as there has been no negligence on the part of the entrepreneur.

Figure 3.11. Structure of *Bai' Inah* Financing

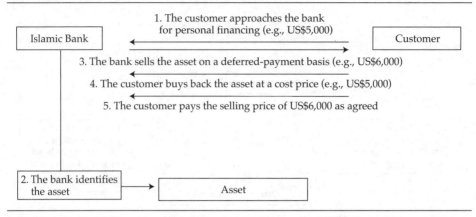

In this form of financing, the bank is the sole contributor of capital and the entrepreneur manages the project. The structure encompasses a two-tier *mudharabah* agreement. The first agreement is between the bank and the investor (who is a different individual from the entrepreneur); the agreement governs the bank's investment of funds in the project and specifies the profit-sharing ratio. The second agreement is between the bank and the entrepreneur; its purpose is to meet the financing needs of the entrepreneur for its *Shari'a*-compliant business activities. Hence, this model comprises both fund gathering (in the form of deposits from investors) and fund use (funds advanced to entrepreneurs). The model is thus based on profit sharing among three parties: the investor, the bank, and the entrepreneur. In a way, the bank acts as a financial intermediary to provide the mechanism for profit-and-loss sharing.

Bai' salam. *Bai' salam* financing is a forward financing transaction frequently used in the agriculture industry. In this structure, the bank purchases specified assets in advance of a predetermined delivery date. Typically, the bank receives a discount for the advance payment plus a profit margin. The quality of the commodities that are being purchased is fully specified so as to leave no room for ambiguity. The agreement is structured to benefit both parties to the transaction (Rosly 2005).

The following mandatory conditions must be met in *bai' salam* arrangements (Gulaid 1995):

- Payment is immediate unless otherwise stipulated in the contract. If not immediate, payment must be made when the seller submits the goods to the buyer.
- Delivery of the goods is at a future date.
- The deliverable goods are specific and can be clearly defined physically and quantitatively.

Qard hassan. *Qard hassan* financing refers to a gratuitous, or charitable, contract in which the borrower is required to repay only the amount borrowed with no profit (markup) to the lender. It may also be described as a form of benevolent financing extended on a goodwill basis. Such loans may be given to the needy for a fixed term.

Qard hassan literally means "good loan." The word "*qard*" is derived from the Arabic "*qirad*," which means "to cut." The use of *qard* refers to the fact that the giving of the loan depletes a certain amount of the lender's property. The word "*hassan*" derives from the Arabic "*ihsan*," which means kindness to others. So, *hassan* is an act that benefits a party other than the party from whom the act proceeds and requires no obligation from the receiving party.

Growth of Islamic Banking

From its inception four decades ago in Egypt, the Islamic banking and finance movement is expected to top US$1 trillion in banking assets by 2010.[8] The Islamic banking industry now encompasses Muslim and non-Muslim participants, including major Western financial institutions, such as Citibank, HSBC, Standard Chartered Bank, the Royal Bank of Scotland, the Australia and New Zealand Banking Group, and JPMorgan Chase.

According to *Asian Banker Journal*, the world's 100 largest wholly Islamic banks held almost US$350 billion in assets in 2006 ("Islamic Banks Are on the Rise" 2008). In 2006, the annual rate of growth of these 100 Islamic banks' assets outpaced asset growth at the world's 100 largest conventional banks by a margin of 26.7 percent versus 19.3 percent. The 100 key Islamic banks are located throughout 24 countries in Asia, the Middle East, and Europe. **Figure 3.12** shows the location of the top 100 Islamic banks and the aggregate size of banking assets managed according to Islamic principles, by country, as of 2007.

Figure 3.12 shows that Iran has a total of 14 state-owned and privately managed banks on the list of the top 100. Combined, the 14 Iranian banks hold nearly half of the 100 largest Islamic banks' assets. Malaysia, which is the dominant Islamic financial market in Asia and which aims to be the international hub for Islamic finance, has 10 full-fledged Islamic banks. Their total assets at the time of the survey (2007), however, accounted for only 5.2 percent of Malaysia's entire banking assets.

Table 3.2 lists and describes the world's top 25 Islamic banks. Bank Melli Iran (BMI) is the largest Islamic bank; it is followed by Saudi Arabia's Al Rajhi Bank.

The Islamic banking landscape in Southeast Asia at year-end 2007 is outlined in **Exhibit 3.1**. In Southeast Asia, the primary banking centers are Singapore and Kuala Lumpur, Malaysia, but Islamic banking services are currently offered in

---

[8]"Morgan Stanley Says ..." (2008).

Brunei, Indonesia, Malaysia, the Philippines, Singapore, and Thailand. According to Kuo (2008), Malaysia, with roughly 15 percent (about US$62 billion) of the entire assets of the Malaysian banking system attributable to *Shari'a*-compliant products, leads the region in terms of total Islamic banking assets.

Figure 3.12.   Location and Aggregate Assets of Top 100 Islamic Banks, 2007

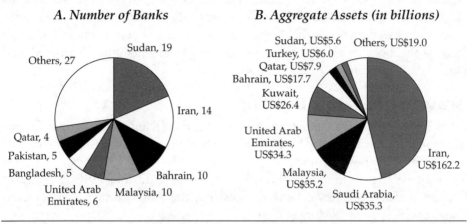

A. Number of Banks

B. Aggregate Assets (in billions)

Source: "Islamic Banks Are on the Rise" (2008).

Exhibit 3.1.   Islamic Banking Presence in Southeast Asia, Year-End 2007

Country	Major Participants	Market Penetration
Brunei	Bank Islam Brunei Darussalam	Market share is 36%; approximately US$4 billion in assets.
Malaysia	11 full-fledged Islamic banks; 7 Islamic banking units of conventional banks; 1 development bank	Market share is 15.4%; approximately US$62 billion in assets.
Philippines	Development Bank of the Philippines, which acquired Al-Amanah Islamic Investment Bank of the Philippines in 2005	Market share and asset size are insignificant.
Indonesia	3 full-fledged Islamic banks; 26 Islamic banking units of conventional banks	Market share is less than 2%; approximately US$3 billion in assets.
Singapore	The Islamic Bank of Asia (established in 2007)	Market share and asset size are insignificant.
Bangladesh	Islami Bank Bangladesh (established in 1983); 5 full-fledged Islamic banks; 20 Islamic banking units of conventional banks	Market share is 25%.
Thailand	Islamic Bank of Thailand	Market share and asset size are insignificant.

Source: Adapted from Kuo (2008).

Table 3.2. Statistics for World's Top 25 Islamic Banks

Rank	Bank	Country	Assets ($ millions)	Islamic Financing ($ millions)	Islamic Deposits ($ millions)	Net Profit After Tax and *Zakat* ($ millions)	ROA (%)	ROE (%)
1	Bank Kerjasama Rakyat Malaysia	Malaysia	7,796.3	5,392.1	6,437.6	109.6	1.4	10.6
2	Maybank Islamic	Malaysia	7,077.1	5,193.5	4,703.5	55.1	0.8	9.7
3	Bank Islam Malaysia	Malaysia	5,533.9	2,460.6	5,098.5	72.7	1.3	24.1
4	Bank Muamalat Malaysia	Malaysia	3,808.8	1,457.8	3,477.0	20.5	0.5	10.1
5	AmIslamic Bank	Malaysia	3,048.4	1,853.1	1,474.7	38.4	1.3	10.1
6	Bank Islam Brunei Darussalam	Brunei	2,910.0	1,295.4	2,293.2	37.2	1.3	7.3
7	RHB Islamic Bank	Malaysia	2,291.5	1,174.5	2,017.6	24.5	1.1	13.3
8	Islami Bank Bangladesh	Bangladesh	2,175.5	1,644.5	1,904.4	20.3	0.9	14.0
9	Faysal Bank	Pakistan	1,894.9	1,222.4	1,463.6	47.1	2.5	32.8
10	Hong Leong Islamic Bank	Malaysia	1,801.8	1,063.3	1,541.7	16.4	0.9	9.5
11	Eoncap Islamic Bank	Malaysia	1,454.1	1,158.0	1,106.1	3.6	0.2	3.1
12	CIMB Islamic Bank	Malaysia	1,261.1	458.8	688.1	4.8	0.4	3.1
13	Affin Islamic Bank	Malaysia	1,106.3	362.1	768.2	10.4	0.9	18.6
14	Bank Syariah Mandiri	Indonesia	1,059.3	792.8	916.3	7.3	0.7	9.4
15	Bank Syariah Muamalat Indonesia	Indonesia	928.0	720.6	781.8	12.0	1.3	13.8
16	Meezan Bank	Pakistan	771.7	443.7	635.4	11.5	1.5	13.3
17	The Islamic Bank of Asia	Singapore	500.0	na	na	na	na	na
18	Oriental Bank Bangladesh	Bangladesh	358.5	277.1	359.2	−6.7	−1.9	31.0
19	Social Investment Bank	Bangladesh	309.4	252.3	240.0	6.8	2.2	27.8
20	Shahjalal Islami Bank	Bangladesh	309.0	224.7	278.9	6.7	2.2	38.4
21	Al-Arafah Islami Bank	Bangladesh	285.1	221.7	231.8	0.8	0.3	5.9
22	Islamic Bank of Thailand	Thailand	149.2	93.3	134.0	−3.9	−2.6	−34.5
23	Bank Syariah Mega Indonesia	Indonesia	91.3	25.0	16.9	0.3	0.4	4.7
24	Bank Islami Pakistan	Pakistan	66.1	17.6	30.4	−0.1	−0.2	−0.4
25	First Dawood Islamic Bank	Pakistan	44.3	0.2	na	na	na	na

Note: Zakat is the religious tithe.
Source: Asian Banker Research (2008).

The Islamic banking share of the total banking system in Indonesia is currently less than 2 percent (US$3 billion), but the Bank of Indonesia, the central bank, aims to increase the market share of Islamic banking in Indonesia to 5 percent by 2010 (Suharmoko 2008). Islamic financing has grown at a competitive clip, increasing by 30 percent in 2007. This growth rate is higher than that of conventional bank lending in Indonesia (which, according to Suharmoko, grew by 25.5 percent in the same year). The Philippines, Singapore, and Thailand each have only one dedicated Islamic bank, and although the share of Islamic banking assets in Brunei is 36 percent, the absolute size, at US$4 billion, is small.

The national Islamic banking markets have been developing at varying paces for different reasons, such as the size of each nation's Muslim population, government initiatives, and the availability of new products and services. Malaysia has perhaps the most developed market in the world for Islamic financial products, partly because of the presence of a significant number of players and partly because of strong government support (Cook 2008). The forecast is for the Islamic banking business in Malaysia to grow to 20 percent of its entire banking system by 2010.[9]

In the oil-rich Gulf Cooperation Council countries—Bahrain, Kuwait, Oman, Qatar, Saudi Arabia, and the United Arab Emirates (UAE)—Islamic banking is expected to grow to 40 percent of the banking system by 2010 from 30 percent in 2005 (Grail Research 2007). Until recently, the Islamic finance industry in the Persian Gulf, a major growth area, has been somewhat fragmented, with each country having a single predominant bank. Doha in Qatar, Manama in Bahrain, and Dubai in the UAE are the main Islamic banking centers in the region. In 2008, Dubai and Saudi Arabia launched large government-backed Islamic banks. This move changed the traditional face of the Islamic banking industry, which has traditionally been populated by many small institutions ("Dubai Forms Islamic Banking Body" 2008).

In the UAE, total Islamic banking assets, including *takaful*, are projected to rise at a 28 percent annual rate to a total of US$87 billion (319 billion dirhams) by 2010, raising the country's global market share of Islamic banking assets to around 11.5 percent (Augustine 2008). An additional goal is to have 20 percent of the nation's banking industry *Shari'a* compliant by 2010 (Grail Research 2007). The share of Islamic banking assets in Kuwait rose from 8.8 percent in 2002 to 13.4 percent in 2008 ("Islamic Banking Statistics" 2008).

In Southeast Asia, Pakistan has experienced solid growth in Islamic banking over the past five years. In 2003, the market share of the Islamic banking system in Pakistan was only 0.5 percent. The country had only one full-fledged Islamic bank and one branch of a conventional bank that offered Islamic banking services. Five years later, Islamic banks in Pakistan had garnered a 4.5 percent market share with

---

[9]Grail Research (2007).

deposits of 160 billion rupees, or US$2.6 billion ("Islamic Banking Captures 4.5% Market Share" 2008). The nation now boasts six full-fledged Islamic banks with 230 branches and 12 conventional banks with 103 Islamic branches. The State Bank of Pakistan, the central bank, plans to strengthen regulation of Islamic banking while expanding market share of the sector to 12 percent by 2012 (Al-Huda 2008).

In Turkey, banks that operate under Islamic principles are known as "participation banks." They are a small but rapidly expanding segment of the Turkish financial sector. As of October 2008, the participation banks—Albaraka Türk, Bank Asya, Kuveyt Türk, and Türkiye Finans—administered about US$21.5 billion in assets, representing 5 percent of the Turkish banking system. The Islamic banking market share in Turkey is expected to double within the next 10 years ("Islamic Finance in Turkey 2009" 2009).

In Europe, London is vying to be the gateway to the continent for Islamic finance. The United Kingdom hosted the first purely Islamic banks in Europe, the Islamic Bank of Britain (which began operations in September 2004) and the European Islamic Investment Bank (which opened its doors in 2006). London is emerging as a hub for Islamic finance because of the financial center's well-established depth and breadth of investment and banking skills and its historical links to the Middle East and Asia.

The future of Islamic banking is bright, with 50 percent of the estimated 1.3 billion to 1.5 billion Muslims worldwide expected to deposit their money in Islamic banks by 2015. The future is even brighter in Asia, where 50–60 percent of all Muslim saving is forecasted to be managed by Islamic financial institutions by the end of the next decade (Murugiah 2007).

Chapter 4. The Islamic Capital Market

The Islamic capital market plays a pivotal role in the growth of Islamic financial institutions. Like any capital market, its primary function is to allow people, companies, and governments with surplus funds to transfer them to people, companies, or governments who need funds. The Islamic capital market functions as a parallel market to the conventional capital market for capital seekers and providers. The Islamic capital market attracts funds from outside as well as inside the market. The international sources might include high-net-worth (HNW) individuals, predominantly Muslims from the oil-rich countries, and others involved in the corporate and business sector. The Islamic capital market does not prohibit participation by non-Muslims, which has increased the growth potential for Islamic products.

Little, if any, consensus exists about the size of the Islamic capital market. Cerulli Associates has estimated the market value of *Shari'a*-compliant assets at year-end 2008 to be US$65 billion, a figure much smaller than often estimated.[10] This amount does not include the market capitalization of equities that are not specifically "Islamic" but in which Islamic financial institutions are permitted to invest (because the business activities of the companies are *Shari'a* compliant). Standard & Poor's (S&P) estimated that as of the third quarter 2008, roughly US$5.2 trillion in market value of *Shari'a*-compliant equities was lost as a result of the global financial crisis that unfolded in 2008.[11] If approximately 40 percent of market value disappeared during the crisis, by inference the current market value would be in the range of US$6 trillion to US$7 trillion. In contrast, as noted, some analysts estimate Islamic banking assets to range between US$500 billion and US$700 billion and expect bank assets to rise to US$1 trillion in 2010 ("Morgan Stanley Says . . ." 2008). Banks have yet to move most of these deposits into managed investments. If the banks require *Shari'a*-compliant products for such investments, the implication is that the Islamic capital market has significant potential for continued growth.

Origin and Growth of the Islamic Capital Market

Although the origins of contemporary Islamic banking and finance may be traced to the early 1960s, the first wave of oil revenues did not wash over the Middle East until the 1970s, when the idea of investing in products conforming to Islamic principles really gained momentum. Individuals in the region began to accumulate large amounts of wealth by the 1980s and began to seek *Shari'a*-compliant financial products in which to invest their savings. Western banks began servicing HNW

---

[10]De Ramos (2009). This article was in the *CFA Institute Financial NewsBrief* of 9 January 2009.
[11]Lacey (2009).

Muslim clients through their Islamic "windows" and were quickly joined in the marketplace by newly organized Islamic banks eager to participate in the growing faith-based demand for *Shari'a*-compliant financial products. As of the end of 2008, the Islamic capital market has largely resulted from retail, not institutional, demand (De Ramos 2009). Institutional demand has developed, however, as Islamic banks and *takaful* (Islamic insurance) operators have sought to invest their surplus funds in *Shari'a*-compliant instruments that are liquid and have long-term maturities to match the long-term liabilities of these institutions.

Through the 1990s, Islamic banking deposits sufficed to provide the capital demanded by the Islamic financial markets, but demand for funds was quickly outstripping the supply of funds. New Islamic financial products that could compete with the flexibility and innovation of conventional financial products were needed, but two factors hindered the ability of the Islamic capital market to deliver such products. The first was that the conventional financial markets were developing with tremendous speed and in many different directions. Challenged to adapt these new products to *Shari'a*, the Islamic financial markets struggled to maintain a competitive pace. The second factor slowing the pace of Islamic capital market development was the conflict surrounding interpretation of what constitutes *Shari'a* compliance (Iqbal and Tsubota 2006; Khan 2006).

Yet, for the Islamic capital market to achieve sustainability, finding new and competitive products was imperative. Deregulation in several Muslim nations opened the door to the creation of two products largely responsible for the serious growth of the Islamic capital market—*Shari'a*-compliant equity funds and *sukuk* (Islamic bonds) (Iqbal and Tsubota 2006; Khan 2006).

Since 1999, the Islamic capital market has attracted non-Muslim as well as Muslim issuers and investors, and it now includes numerous products that can replicate the returns and characteristics of conventional financial products. In addition to equity and bond products, the market has expanded to include exchange-traded funds, derivatives, swaps, unit trusts, real estate investment trusts (REITs), commodity funds, and a range of Islamic indices and index products. The Islamic capital market comprises active primary and secondary markets that deal in the Islamic products described in this section.

Overview of the Islamic Capital Market

Not all the financial products discussed in this overview are acceptable to all Muslim investors. The controversy over what is and what is not *Shari'a* compliant is a byproduct of the existence of different schools of Islamic thought. No single body is currently in place to mediate these differences of opinion.

The Islamic Equity Market. Islamic equities are shares of *halal* companies—that is, securities of companies operating in activities permissible under *Shari'a* principles and approved and periodically reviewed by *Shari'a* scholars through a process known as Islamic stock screening. For a company to be considered *halal*, the majority of its revenues must be primarily derived from activities other than the trading of alcohol, arms, tobacco, pork, pornography, or gambling or from profits associated with charging interest on loans.

The determination of *Shari'a* compliance rests with the judgment of Islamic scholars. In Malaysia, one of the most innovative providers of financial products, the body of Islamic scholars is the Malaysia Securities Commission *Shari'a* Advisory Council (SAC). Malaysia is one of only a few nations that has established a single governing body for this purpose. Other nations' decision making regarding *Shari'a* screening procedures is much more fragmented. The SAC has enumerated detailed criteria to be used in screening companies for compliance with Islamic principles. The SAC states that non-*halal* activities include manufacturing and trading of non-*halal* goods; banking and financing involving interest or usury; hotels and resorts involved in the sale of liquor or alcoholic beverages; gambling or related activities; and activities involving elements of uncertainty (*gharar*).

The Malaysian stock-screening criteria are similar to the criteria adopted by the *Financial Times* (FTSE) and Dow Jones Islamic Market Indexes series, the major indices that provide Islamic screening filters.[12] An exception, however, is that the Malaysian criteria specifically prohibit companies involved in meat production or sale if the animals are not slaughtered according to Islamic rites. (The major Islamic equity indices are discussed in greater detail later in this chapter.)

Following the approach of these two indices, the SAC determines compliance on the basis of the core activities of a company; it does not exclude a company if a minor portion of its business is derived from involvement in *haram* (not permissible) activities. The SAC has also adopted positive *Shari'a* screening criteria that require that the public perception or image of a company be good and that its core activities have importance to the Muslim *ummah*, the overarching global Muslim community. The company's guiding principles should conform to *maslahah*, the beliefs of Muslims. Companies that serve the non-Muslim community, such as those operated by the Chinese population in Malaysia, are regarded as legitimate for investment purposes as long as their business activities are consistent with activities customarily accepted by Muslims.

The *Shari'a* stock-screening criteria used by Malaysia's SAC, as well as other screening entities, are essentially qualitative, but some quantitative criteria are also used. Quantitative criteria include, for example, the calculation of certain financial ratios, such as the proportion of interest-bearing debt to assets or total debt to the average market capitalization of the company over a period of 12 months. (In Malaysia, screening by financial ratios is not used.)

---

[12]Descriptions of the FTSE *Shari'ah*-compliant indices can be found at www.ftse.com/Indices/index.jsp. A guide to the Dow Jones Islamic Market Indexes can be found at www.djindexes.com/mdsidx/?event=showIslamic.

The Islamic equity investment market is growing at a much faster rate than the overall Islamic sector as a whole because it started from a lower base. The total of funds under management in the Islamic finance sector is estimated at US$1 trillion. Only about an estimated US$20 billion of this is in equities, however, which is modest in comparison with the conventional equity sector with its market capitalization of almost US$2 trillion. Global conventional equities are about US$20 trillion, even after the crash (Parker 2008a).

Malaysia is seen as aggressive in listing Islamic equities; more than 80 percent of the stocks listed on the Bursa Malaysia are classified as *Shari'a*-approved by the SAC. These securities have a total market capitalization of 426.4 billion Malaysian ringgits (RM), or US$129 billion, which is 64.2 percent of the total Malaysian stock market as of December 2008 (Ngadimon 2009). In Kuwait, Islamic and *Shari'a*-compliant companies make up 57 percent of the country's total market capitalization ("Islamic, Sharia Firms . . ." 2009). Despite the recent huge decline in the financial markets, Islamic equity funds have been attracting global investors and more and more financial institutions are offering such funds to meet investor demand.

Islamic Bond (*Sukuk*) Market

One of the fastest growing sectors in the Islamic capital market is the *sukuk*, or Islamic asset-backed bond, market. The *sukuk* market grew at about an 84 percent per year compound rate between 2001 and 2007 and was estimated to have a market value of US$80 billion to US$90 billion before the 2008 market crisis (Cook 2008). Over the first eight months of 2008, global *sukuk* issuance totaled roughly US$14 billion, down from US$23 billion for the same period a year earlier, mainly because of the global credit crunch ("Sukuk Issuance . . ." 2008). *Sukuk* are issued primarily by corporations, although sovereign issuers are becoming more common than in the past. About half of outstanding *sukuk*, mainly large U.S. dollar–based issues and Malaysian debt, are actively traded in the secondary market.

Sukuk are a relatively new financial instrument, first issued in the late 1990s. *Sukuk* were created in response to a need for *Shari'a*-compliant medium-term to long-term debt-like instruments that would have good liquidity in the marketplace (Iqbal and Tsubota 2006). The word "*sukuk*" is the plural of the Arabic word "*sakk*," which means "certificate," so *sukuk* may be described as certificates of trust for the ownership of an asset, or certificates of usufruct. *Sukuk* differ from conventional bonds in that they do not pay interest. Islam forbids the payment of interest, but a financial obligation or instrument that is linked to the performance of a real asset is acceptable.

Sukuk returns are tied to the cash streams generated by underlying assets held in special purpose vehicles (SPVs). The cash stream can be in the form of profit from a sale, profit from a rental, or a combination of the two. The conventional asset securitization process is used in structuring *sukuk*. An SPV is created to acquire the assets that will collateralize the *sukuk* and to issue financial claims on those assets over the defined term of the *sukuk*. A trust financing, or *mudharabah*, contract is used to create the SPV, otherwise known as a special purpose *mudharabah* (SPM). The asset collateral must be *Shari'a* compliant (Iqbal and Tsubota 2006). *Sukuk* are, therefore, monetized real assets that enjoy significant liquidity and are easily transferred and traded in financial markets. A *sukuk* issue can be structured in a variety of ways and can offer fixed- and variable-income options.

Several classes of assets typically collateralize *sukuk* issues. The first class has financial claims arising from a spot sale (*salam*) or a deferred-payment (*bai' mu'ajjal*) and/or deferred-delivery (*bai' salam*) sale. These securities are typically short term in nature, ranging from three months to one year, and are used to finance commodity trading. Because the risk-and-return characteristics of the structure are somewhat delinked from the risk-and-return characteristics of the underlying asset, the Gulf Cooperation Council (GCC) countries (see Exhibit 1.2) hold that trading these *sukuk* in the secondary market involves *riba*; hence, it is prohibited. Therefore, *salam*-based *sukuk* are typically held to maturity (Iqbal and Tsubota 2006).

A second class of assets that collateralize *sukuk* is leased, or *ijarah*-based, assets. The cash flows generated by the lease-and-buyback agreement, a combination of rental and principal payments, are passed through to investors. *Ijarah*-based *sukuk* have medium- to long-term maturities (Iqbal and Tsubota 2006), carry a put option, and can be traded in the secondary market. This type of *sukuk* has gained increasing acceptance by *Shari'a* scholars, particularly those from Middle Eastern countries. Recent successful issues include those by the Malaysian-based companies Al-'Aqar Capital (RM500 million, or US$153 million) and Menara ABS (RM1.1 billion, or US$337 million).

The structure of the *ijarah sukuk* is depicted in **Figure 4.1** and consists of the following steps:

1. The seller sells the assets to the issuer for a purchase price based on the value of the assets.

Figure 4.1. Structure of *Ijarah Sukuk*

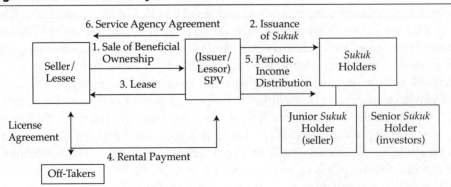

---

2. To finance the purchase, the issuer raises *sukuk* of an equivalent amount through a combination of senior and junior *sukuk*. The senior *sukuk* are subscribed to by the investors, whereas the junior *sukuk* are solely subscribed to by the seller. (The *sukuk* represent the beneficial rights in the assets whereby the *sukuk* holders have an undivided proportionate beneficial interest in the assets. The issuer declares a trust via a trust declaration over the assets for the benefit of the *sukuk* investors. The *sukuk* investors, therefore, have a pro rata undivided beneficial ownership of the assets.)

3. Subsequent to the purchase, the issuer leases the acquired assets to the lessee under *ijarah* agreement(s) for an *ijarah* term of up to, perhaps, eight years.

4. The lessee makes *ijarah* rental payments to the issuer from the income received from the "off-takers" (tenants/customers of the financed project) arising from the license agreement.

5. The *ijarah* rental payments for the assets received by the issuer from the lessor are then distributed to the *sukuk* holders as a periodic income-distribution payment in proportion to their holdings in the *sukuk*.

6. The seller, in the capacity of service agent, enters into a service agency agreement with the issuer to provide major maintenance services and to maintain insurance for the assets.

A third class of assets used to collateralize *sukuk* is an asset supported by a *musyarakah* (joint venture) contract; these issues are called "investment *sukuk*" or "*sukuk al-musyarakah*." The structure, which is depicted in **Figure 4.2,** involves the issuer entering into a joint-venture *musyarakah* agreement with another party (the investor) and incorporates the use of an SPV. *Musyarakah* involves a partnership arrangement between two parties or more to finance a business venture to which all parties contribute capital, either in cash or in kind, for the purpose of financing the venture (refer to Chapters 2 and 3).

The bulk of *sukuk* have been issued in the Middle East and Malaysia, although the German state of Saxony and the World Bank have also issued *sukuk*. Malaysia offered the first sovereign *sukuk* in 2002. In March 2008, the first sovereign *sukuk* were listed on the London Stock Exchange (LSE) by Bahrain, which chose the LSE for listing its second *sukuk* issue (the first having been issued in Luxembourg in 2004) in order to encourage European and conventional investors to buy the *sukuk*. More than 50 percent of the issue was bought by European investors, with the remainder purchased primarily by banks based in the Middle East. The US$350 million Bahrain issue raised the market value of *sukuk* listed on the LSE to US$11 billion (Al Maraj 2008). In addition to Bahrain and Malaysia, Qatar and Pakistan have also issued sovereign *sukuk*. *Sukuk* have also been issued in the United States, with the first issue being that of the Texas-based oil and gas company East Cameron Partners—a US$166 million deal in June 2006.

Figure 4.2. Structure of *Sukuk Al-Musyarakah* Contract

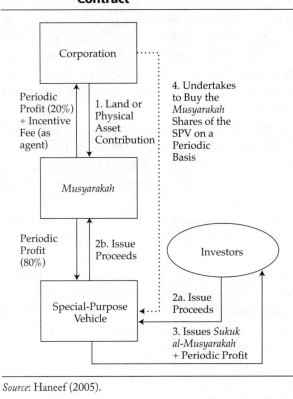

Source: Haneef (2005).

The majority of *sukuk* are issued in U.S. dollars, have maturities of three to five years, and have, each, a total issue size of only several hundred million dollars. Most are not rated by any of the big three rating agencies. When *sukuk* are rated, however, the depth of analysis is often handicapped by a lack of transparency. As a result of small issue size and limited ability to assess creditworthiness, most *sukuk* offer little secondary market liquidity. The NASDAQ Dubai, with 20 issues totaling US$16 billion as of year-end 2008, is the largest *sukuk* listing platform.[13]

Nearly 70 percent of global outstanding *sukuk* have originated in Malaysia. **Figure 4.3** depicts the growth of the Malaysian *sukuk* market from 2001 to 2007. In 2007, the Malaysian market accounted for about half of the US$51.5 billion *sukuk* issued. The Malaysia Securities Commission approved 22 *sukuk* issues worth RM17.7 billion, or US$5.5 billion, in the first half of 2008, which accounted for 31 percent of total corporate bond issuance approved in Malaysia during the period.

---

[13]See the NASDAQ Dubai at www.nasdaqdubai.com/home/home.html.

Figure 4.3. *Sukuk* Issuance in Malaysia, 2001–07

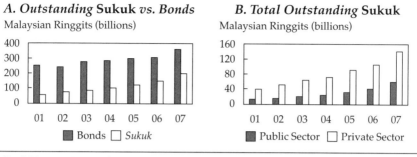

Source: Bank Negara Malaysia (2008).

Islamic Derivatives Market

A derivative, a financial instrument whose value is a function of the value of another asset, typically takes the form of a contract in which the investor promises to deliver, or take delivery of, an asset at a specific date and at a specific price. Conventional derivatives include call and put options, futures, forwards, and swaps and are used for hedging, arbitrage, and speculation. Islamic finance allows derivatives for the first two purposes—hedging and arbitrage—but prohibits their use for speculation or gambling (*maisir*). As long as *riba* (interest) and *gharar* (uncertainty) are avoided, the Islamic derivative structure used in hedging and arbitrage enjoys significant freedom of design.

The size of the Islamic derivative market is not known but is quite small. The development of Islamic derivative products will bring effective risk management to Islamic financial market participants.

Islamic derivative products include the structured *murabahah* deposit, structured options that operate on the principle of *wa'd* (promise), profit rate swaps, and cross-currency swaps, such as the foreign exchange (FX) *wa'd* (a *Shari'a*-complaint FX option) and the Islamic FX outright (a *Shari'a*-compliant FX forward contract that locks in the price at which an entity can buy or sell a currency at a future date).

Islamic derivatives are based on contracts that are supported by the principles of *bai' salam*, *bai' istisna*, or *urbun*. *Bai' salam* allows delivery of an asset at a future date at today's price and is similar to a forward contract except that in a *bai' salam* contract, only one party is deferring his or her obligation under the contract. *Bai' salam* requires that the asset be defined in quantity, quality, and workmanship and that the delivery date be fixed. The asset must be tangible, with the exception of gold and silver because these precious metals are regarded as money. Neither contracting party may rescind the contract unless the asset controlled by the contract is found to be defective.

A *bai' istisna* contract is a deferred-sale (a manufacture per specifications and sale) contract in which the price of an asset is paid in installments as the contract term progresses. The *bai' istisna* contract is typically used to finance manufactured assets and, unlike the *bai' salam* contract, can be canceled unilaterally if the manufacturing process has not yet begun (see Chapters 2 and 3 for details).

Urbun refers to a sale in which the buyer deposits money in advance with the seller as partial payment and agrees that if the buyer cancels the contract, the deposit will be forfeited and kept by the seller. If the buyer eventually decides to proceed with the transaction, the payment terms are reduced by the amount of the initial deposit. Some schools of Islam, such as Hanafi, Shafi'i, and Maliki, find *urbun*-based contracts unacceptable on the ground that they involve *gharar* (uncertainty). The Hanbali school, however, believes an *urbun* transaction is *halal* (permissible).

Islamic Swap Market

The Islamic swap market is a subset of the overall Islamic derivative market. A swap is a derivative instrument that is used to transfer risk. The two major Islamic swap structures are the profit rate swap, which is similar to a conventional interest rate swap, and a cross-currency swap. Total return swaps are also being used.

Profit Rate Swap. The Islamic profit rate swap is used as a hedge against fluctuations in borrowing rates. The swap is an agreement to exchange fixed for floating profit rates between two parties and is implemented through the execution of a series of underlying contracts to trade certain assets under the *Shari'a* principles of *bai* and *bai' bithaman ajil* (see Chapter 3 for the mechanics of these contracts). **Figure 4.4** depicts the structure of an Islamic profit rate swap.[14] Each party's payment obligation is computed from a different pricing formula. The notional principal is never exchanged because it is netted out under the principle of *muqasah* (set-offs) (Sukri and Hussin 2006).

The profit rate swap gives Islamic investors a tool to help them match financing rates with investment return rates, lower their costs of funding, restructure an existing debt without altering their balance sheets, and manage exposure to interest rate movements.

The first Islamic profit rate swap was pioneered by CIMB Islamic in 2005. In 2007, Deutsche Bank closed a US$500 million profit rate collar swap with Dubai Islamic Bank, which stretched the boundaries of Islamic derivative products farther than ever before.

---

[14]The presentation by Ghani (2004) entitled "Islamic Profit Rate Swap: Its Mechanics and Objectives" on the Resources page of the Islamic Interbank Money Market website (http://iimm.bnm.gov.my/index.php?ch=20&pg=66) contains excellent information about the structure of profit rate swaps, including additional figures.

Figure 4.4. Structure of Islamic Profit Rate Swap

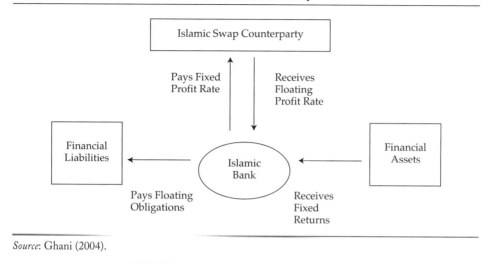

Source: Ghani (2004).

Cross-Currency Swap. The Islamic cross-currency swap is a vehicle through which investors can transfer the risk of currency fluctuation that is inherent in their investment or inventory positions. The structure involves two simultaneous *murabahah* transactions—one is a term *murabahah* and the other, a reverse *murabahah* (see Chapter 2 for the mechanics of a *murabahah*-based contract). The parties to the swap agree to sell *Shari'a*-compliant assets to each other for immediate delivery but on deferred-payment terms in different currencies.

The first cross-currency swap was done in July 2006 for US$10 million between Standard Chartered Bank Malaysia and Bank Muamalat Malaysia.

Islamic Unit Trusts

An Islamic unit trust is similar to a conventional unit trust in the United Kingdom and an open-end mutual fund in the United States except that the Islamic unit trust invests only in *Shari'a*-compliant securities; that is, the unit trust manager gives precedence to securities (stocks or bonds) of Islamic banks and financial institutions, securities of companies operated in accordance with Islamic principles, and securities included in Islamic equity indices. Islamic mutual funds (unit trusts) vary by investment type and financing method (*murabahah*, *musyarakah*, *bai' salam*, *bai' istisna*, or *ijarah*); field of investment (public works, real estate, or leasing); period of investment (short, medium, or long term); risk involved (low, medium, or high risk); and whether they are open or closed funds (Tayar 2006).

The contract governing the exchange of units between the unit trust manager and the investor usually conforms to the principle of *bai' al-naqdi* (buying and selling on a cash basis). When an investor purchases a unit of the trust, the investor is actually sharing pro rata with other investors in ownership of the assets held by the trust. The manager receives a management fee under the concept of *al-ujrah* (or fee) for managing the unit trust.

An equity unit trust is the most common type of Islamic unit trust, but corporate and sovereign *sukuk* (bond) unit trusts are also available. Certain equity unit trusts invest in assets that closely track a particular index and are known as "index trackers." Specialist unit trusts invest in a single industry or similar group of industries. Balanced funds incorporate both equity and *sukuk* securities and are rebalanced periodically to retain the initial asset allocation. Islamic fund managers have less autonomy than conventional fund managers because they are usually accountable to a *Shari'a* committee or adviser who rules on the screening criteria for stock selection and how the criteria are to be interpreted in changing market conditions and company circumstances.

Muslims can, of course, make investments directly and manage their own portfolios rather than investing indirectly through fund management groups and incurring management charges. The search costs are higher for Muslim direct investors, however, if they want to satisfy themselves that the companies or businesses they are investing in are acceptable under *Shari'a*.

In addition, Islamic unit trusts may offer a better risk profile than Islamic investment products that expose investors to the counterparty risk of a bank ("Islamic Unit Trusts" 2007). For example, investors who place their money in restricted or *mudharabah* investment accounts, in which legal ownership lies with the bank, are exposed to the risk that the counterparty bank will go bankrupt. A unit trust structure in which investors own a pro rata share of the investment portfolio, however, does not expose the investor to such counterparty risk. **Figure 4.5** compares the two forms of investment account.

The first Islamic equity unit trust, Tabung Ittikal Arab-Malaysian, was established in Malaysia in 1993 (AMMB 2006). In recent years, growth in the equity funds market has been strong, particularly in Malaysia because of the country's tax incentives and favorable regulatory environment, although Saudi Arabia is the largest Islamic equity funds market in terms of asset size and number of funds. According to Cerulli Associates, as of year-end 2008, approximately 500 *Shari'a*-compliant fund products were in the market, totaling US$35 billion (De Ramos 2009).

These data are consistent with data provided by Eurekahedge, which reports that the number of Islamic unit trust and investment funds stood at 504 worldwide as of April 2008, with total assets under management (AUM) at US$33.9 billion. **Figure 4.6** shows that over the past decade (December 1997–April 2008), the number of Islamic funds worldwide grew at an annualized rate of 26 percent. In 2007, 111 new funds entered the market, up from 77 new entries in 2006.

Figure 4.5. Comparison of *Mudharabah* Investment Account and Islamic Unit Trust

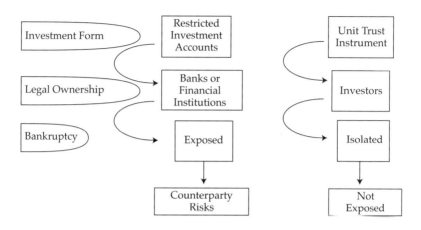

Source: "Islamic Unit Trusts" (2007).

Figure 4.6. Growth in Islamic Unit Trusts, 1997–April 2008

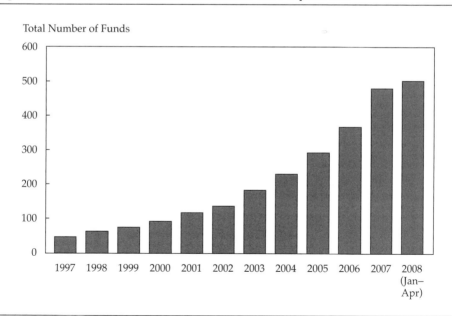

Source: AmBank Group (2008).

The global Islamic fund industry is dominated by Saudi Arabia and Malaysia, which account for, respectively, 26 percent and 25 percent of the total number of funds as of April 2008. In terms of AUM, the two countries together held nearly three-quarters (US$24.5 billion) of the market.[15] In terms of number of funds, the countries with the next largest presence are Kuwait (15 percent market share), the United Arab Emirates (7.7 percent), and Indonesia (5 percent); in terms of AUM, the market share was Kuwait (10 percent), United Arab Emirates (6 percent), and Indonesia (less than 1 percent).

In the three-year period from 2005 to 2007, Saudi Arabia, Malaysia, and Kuwait hosted the launch of the greatest number of new funds, with Kuwait's total rising from 7 new funds in 2005 to 24 new funds in 2007. Saudi Arabia dominated in 2005 with 19 new funds, but in 2007, it dropped to third place, with 17 new funds, behind Malaysia and Kuwait with, respectively, 26 and 24 funds.

Equity funds are the most popular type of Islamic fund. Of the 504 funds existing as of April 2008, more than half (278) were equity funds, and they had total AUM equal to US$18.3 billion. The money market and commodity trading fund mandate was a distant second at 70 funds (14 percent) with AUM of nearly US$11 billion (32 percent). Jockeying for third place were balanced funds (with the number of funds at 55 [11 percent market share] and AUM of approximately US$1.1 billion [3 percent market share]), real estate and private equity funds (at 45 [9 percent] with AUM of approximately US$2.3 billion [6.7 percent]), and debt funds (at 36 [7 percent] with AUM of approximately US$1.1 billion [3 percent]).

Table 4.1 shows the number of new funds launched, by mandate, from 2000 through the first four months of 2008. In 2007, money market and commodity trading funds were the most popular type of new fund. Although the total number of new funds has risen dramatically over the past several years, the breakdown of new issuance by type of fund has remained relatively consistent. In 2007, equity funds made up 63 of the total 112 funds launched, thus making this category the most popular for number of funds launched.

As of April 2008, fund investments were geographically distributed as follows. Investments in the Middle East/Africa region dominated, with 155 funds and US$22 billion in AUM (64.8 percent of the total Islamic fund asset size of US$34 billion). Asia Pacific funds totaled 184 (36.5 percent) with AUM of US$5 billion (roughly 15 percent). In third place were funds with a global mandate, which consisted of 117 funds (23 percent) with AUM of US$4.9 billion (roughly 15 percent), and in fourth place were funds with investments in North America, which consisted of 32 funds (6.35 percent) with AUM of US$1.5 billion (roughly 5 percent). Europe and the emerging markets represented, respectively, 11 funds with AUM of US$143 million and 5 funds with AUM of US$260 million.

---

[15]Data in this section are from AmBank Group (2008).

Table 4.1. Islamic Mutual Funds Launched, by Mandate: 2000–April 2008

Calendar Year	Equity	Money Market and Commodities Trading	Balanced	Real Estate and Private Equity	Debt Securities	Others
2000	0	2	1	2	1	13
2001	1	5	6	1	3	9
2002	0	3	3	1	1	10
2003	2	5	9	4	5	22
2004	1	7	6	7	4	21
2005	1	8	7	9	8	28
2006	4	5	9	6	5	48
2007	6	17	9	8	8	63
2008 (Jan to Apr)	2	3	7	1	1	10

Source: AmBank Group 2008.

Table 4.2 shows the changing regional mandates of newly established funds from 2000 through the first four months of 2008. In 2007, the most popular new mandate was the Asia Pacific region, with 38 new funds out of a total of 111 launched—nearly one-third of all new funds. The second most popular mandate was global, followed by Middle East/Africa funds.

Islamic Exchange-Traded Funds

An exchange-traded fund (ETF) is an open-ended fund composed of quoted securities—stocks or bonds—that are selected to closely mimic a benchmark, rather like an index-tracking mutual fund. Unlike an index mutual fund, an ETF is bought and sold on an exchange. The price of an ETF should closely track the weighted

Table 4.2. Islamic Mutual Funds Launched, by Geographical Area

Calendar Year	Asia Pacific	Emerging Markets	Europe	Global	Middle East/ Africa	North America
2000	5	0	4	7	0	3
2001	14	0	1	2	7	1
2002	8	0	0	4	6	0
2003	17	0	4	11	13	2
2004	23	0	1	6	13	3
2005	23	1	4	29	0	4
2006	28	2	2	16	25	4
2007	38	2	8	36	27	0
2008 (Jan to Apr)	8	1	8	2	4	0

Source: AmBank Group 2008.

net asset values of its portfolio of securities throughout the trading day. An Islamic ETF is structured exactly like a conventional ETF except that the benchmark used in constructing the fund is an index of *Shari'a*-compliant securities; that is, the index includes only those securities that have passed Islamic filters to ensure that companies are primarily engaged in permissible business activities and do not have high levels of debt.

Islamic ETFs made their debut in February 2006. Although it is a nascent market, Islamic ETFs have been issued by several major players in the global capital markets, such as iShares, BNP Paribas Bank, Daiwa Asset Management, and Deutsche Bank. As of year-end 2008, the three iShares ETFs totaled US$25.8 million.[16] **Exhibit 4.1** lists several major Islamic ETFs. JETS (Javelin Exchange Traded Shares), which is the first Islamic ETF expected to be issued in the United States and is to be made available by Javelin Investment Management and the Dow Jones Islamic Market (DJIM) International Index Fund, has been filed with the U.S. SEC and is anticipated to be launched on NYSE Arca in early 2009.[17]

Figure 4.7 illustrates the structure of an ETF. Participating dealers or market makers deliver the exchange-traded securities selected for the ETF to the fund manager in exchange for units in the ETF. The ETF units, representing an ownership interest in the basket of securities, are then sold to investors via an exchange. When ETF units are redeemed, market makers return them to the fund manager in exchange for a proportionate share of the basket of securities.

Exhibit 4.1. Principal Islamic ETFs

DJIM Turkey ETF	DJIM Turkey	Bizim Menkul	Feb 2006/Istanbul
EasyETF DJIM Titan 100	DJIM Titan 100	BNP Paribas	Feb 2007/Zurich
MSCI World Islamic	MSCI World Islamic	iShares	Dec 2007/London
MSCI Emerging Markets Islamic	MSCI Emerging Markets Islamic	iShares	Dec 2007/London
MSCI USA Islamic	MSCI USA Islamic	iShares	Dec 2007/London
MyETF DJIM *Malaysia Titans 25*	DJIM *Malaysia Titans 25*	CIMB	Jan 2008/Kuala Lumpur
Db x-tracker DJIM Titan 100	DJIM Titan 100	Deutsche Bank	Aug 2008/London
Diawa FTSE Shariah Japan 100	FTSE Shariah Japan 100	Daiwa Asset Management	Jun 2008/Singapore

[16]See the iShares website at http://us.ishares.com/home.htm.
[17]Rosenbaum (2008).

Figure 4.7.   Structure of ETF

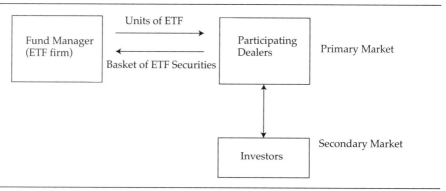

The advantages of ETFs from the investor's viewpoint include tax efficiency, low cost, transparency, trading flexibility, and diversification. ETFs are often used as a hedging instrument as well as a means to obtain access to an asset class cheaply and quickly.

Islamic REITs

Islamic REITs (I-REITs) are similar to conventional REITs. They are typically structured as property trusts except that they must hold investments that adhere to the principles of *Shari'a*. This requirement means that lease financing (*ijarah*) is used in lieu of an outright purchase of property. The economic, legal, and tax ramifications are effectively the same as in a conventional REIT.

An Islamic REIT invests primarily in physical real estate, but it may also hold *sukuk*, private companies whose main assets comprise real estate, *Shari'a*-compliant securities of property and nonproperty companies, units of other I-REITS, *Shari'a*-compliant short-term deposits, and cash. I-REITs vary from country to country. The Malaysia Securities Commission defines an I-REIT as "an investment vehicle that proposes to invest at least 50 percent of its total assets in real estate, whether through direct ownership or through a single purpose company whose principal asset comprises a real asset" (Securities Commission 2005). The structure of an Islamic REIT is illustrated in **Figure 4.8**.

The key benefits of I-REITS are similar to those of conventional REITs and include the following advantages over physical properties (Jaafar 2007):

- higher current yields because of the requirement to distribute at least 90 percent of income annually,
- lower transaction costs and greater liquidity because most REITs are listed and traded on stock exchanges,
- scalability, unlike property investment companies, and
- diversification across properties with different lease periods and geographical locations.

Figure 4.8. Structure of an Islamic REIT

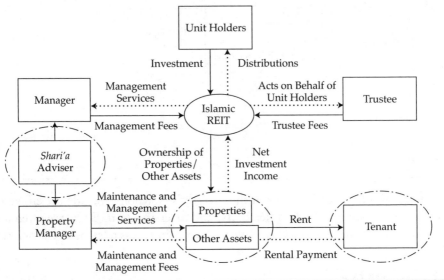

Source: Jaafar (2007).

I-REIT returns are earned through rental income, capital appreciation of physical property, and securities held as investments. I-REIT investments must be reviewed, monitored, and approved as complying with *Shari'a* principles by a *Shari'a* committee or adviser. In addition, an I-REIT is required to use a *takaful* (Islamic insurance) scheme to insure the real estate. The Malaysia Securities Commission permits up to 20 percent of REIT rental income to be derived from nonpermissible, or non-*Shari'a*-compliant, activities.

The first Islamic REIT, the Malaysian Al-'Aqar KPJ Healthcare REIT, was launched in Malaysia in 2006 with initial issuance of US$130 million (Lerner 2006). Malaysia was the first country, in 2005, to issue *Shari'a*-compliant REIT guidelines. Malaysian issues are listed and traded on Bursa Malaysia and may also be dual listed (that is, listed on Bursa Malaysia and on another exchange). They are liquid securities that trade as any other stock trades. Having been in existence for only two years, the Islamic REIT market still remains quite small.

Islamic Commodity Funds

An Islamic commodity fund, like all Islamic financial products, must comply with *Shari'a* principles; therefore, commodity fund transactions are governed by the following rules (Usmani, no date):

- The commodity must be owned by the seller at the time of sale because short selling is not permitted under *Shari'a* but forward sales, allowed only in the case of *bai' salam* and *bai' istisna*, are permitted.

- The commodity traded must be *halal* (permissible), which means that dealing in, for example, wine and pork is prohibited.
- The seller must have physical or constructive possession (that is, actual control without actually having physical control) of the commodity to be sold.
- The price of the commodity must be fixed and known to the parties involved.
- Any price that is uncertain, or that is determinable by an uncertain event, renders the sale invalid.

The performance of commodity prices in the years leading up to the 2008 bull market peak has been attributed to favorable demand conditions for raw materials and, in most cases, inelastic supply responses because of years of underinvestment in production capacity. This bull market was followed by an extremely sharp commodity price decline in 2008–2009, illustrating how volatile and unpredictable commodity prices are.

The advantage of a commodity fund is that it is not highly correlated with equity and fixed-income asset classes. Hence, it acts as a diversifying asset, particularly when the other assets held are equities and bonds (but commodities did not diversify equity risk in 2008–2009). A commodity fund aims to provide investors with regular income over the life of the fund—income that is linked to the performance of commodities through investments that conform with *Shari'a* principles. The commodity funds generate income from the potential appreciation in commodity prices.

Islamic Indices

The Dow Jones Islamic Market Index and TII-FTSE Islamic Index, launched in 1999 and 2000, respectively, were the first global Islamic benchmarks. Since that time, Morgan Stanley Capital International (MSCI) and S&P have also developed Islamic indices.

In 2006, S&P began offering the S&P 500 Sharia Index, the S&P Europe 350 Sharia Index, and the S&P Japan 500 Sharia Index. At the initial launch of the S&P series, 295 stocks in the S&P 500 Sharia were deemed to be *Shari'a* compliant; 139 stocks, in the S&P Europe 350; and 286, in the S&P Japan 500. In 2007, MSCI entered the market with three indices—the MSCI Emerging Markets Islamic Index, MSCI USA Islamic Index, and MSCI World Islamic Index.

S&P followed the launch of their three broad indices with a series of narrower indices in 2007. The S&P/International Financial Corporation Investable GCC indices include six *Shari'a*-compliant country indices (one for each of the six Gulf Cooperation Council countries of Bahrain, Kuwait, Oman, Qatar, Saudi Arabia, and the UAE), a composite that excludes Saudi Arabia, and a composite that includes Saudi Arabia. The S&P Pan Asia Shariah Index includes *Shari'a*-compliant securities in China, Hong Kong, India, Malaysia, the Philippines, Singapore, South Korea, Taiwan, and Thailand. To be included, a stock must have at least US$1 billion in float-adjusted market capitalization, and to expedite the *Shari'a* screening process, only the top 15 stocks in each country are evaluated.

By year-end 2008, the Dow Jones Islamic Market Index family had expanded to incorporate 70 indices at the regional, country, industry, and market-capitalization levels, including the markets of the United States, Europe and the Eurozone, the Asia Pacific region, the BRIC countries (Brazil, Russia, India, and China), and Canada, among others.[18]

The FTSE family of Islamic indices at year-end 2008 included the global FTSE Shariah All-World Index of large- and mid-cap stocks, begun in 2007, and the FTSE regional family of *Shari'a*-compliant indices, which includes (1) the first of the FTSE SGX (Singapore Stock Exchange) index series—namely, the FTSE SGX Asia Shariah 100 Index, which was launched in 2003 and includes 50 of the largest Japanese companies and 50 of the largest companies from Singapore, Korea, Taiwan, and Hong Kong; (2) the FTSE DIFX (Dubai International Financial Exchange) index series (soon to be renamed to reflect the Dubai exchange's new name, NASDAQ Dubai), which were the first tradable indices in the GCC region and which include the FTSE DIFX Kuwait 15 Shariah Index and FTSE DIFX Qatar 10 Shariah Index; and (3) the FTSE Bursa Malaysia index series, which includes the FTSE Bursa Malaysia EMAS (Exchange Main Board All-Shares) Shariah Index and the FTSE Bursa Malaysia Hijrah Shariah Index.

The Jakarta Islamic Index, which contains 30 companies listed on the Indonesia Stock Exchange, has been available since 2000.

Table 4.3 compares the quantitative screens of the four major Islamic index families.

Table 4.3. Quantitative Screens of Major Islamic Index Families

Financial Category	DJIM	FTSE	S&P	MSCI
Debt	33%	33%	33%	33.33%
	Trlg 12m avg mkt cap	Total assets	Mkt value equity	Total assets
Receivables	33%	50%	49%	70%
	Trlg 12m avg mkt cap	Total assets	Mkt value equity	Total assets
Cash	33%	33%	33%	33.33%
	Trlg 12m avg mkt cap	Total assets	Mkt value equity	Total assets

Note: "Trlg" stands for "trailing."

Source: Mansor (2008) from "Guide to the Dow Jones Islamic Market Indexes" (November 2007), "Ground Rules for the Management of FTSE Shariah Global Equity Index Series Version 1.2" (March 2008), "S&P Shariah Indices Index Methodology" (June 2007), and "MSCI Islamic Index Series Methodology" (April 2007).

---

[18] An overview of the Dow Jones Islamic Market Indexes may be found at www.djindexes.com/mdsidx/?event=showIslamicOverView.

These indices are not accepted as *halal* by all Islamic scholars. Because the screening criteria allow debt ratios of up to 33 percent, certain Islamic scholars argue that accepting the indices is akin to declaring a food *halal* if it contains only a small quantity of pork.

Continued Growth in the Islamic Capital Market

Financial products that barely existed a few years ago have now penetrated the broad Islamic capital market. But some products, such as Islamic hedge funds, remain controversial in large portions of the Muslim community, which view hedge fund activities as simply simulating short selling in ways designed to be compatible with *Shari'a*. The five schools of Islam vary in their definition of what complies with *Shari'a*, which raises a key obstacle to the creation of universally acceptable Islamic hedging schemes.

Nevertheless, two investment firms, Barclays Capital and Shariah Capital, have launched a *Shari'a*-compliant hedge fund product that replicates shorting by using the *urbun* contract—that is, a sale in which the buyer deposits money in advance (Parker 2008b). In Islamic finance, an asset should be owned before it is sold, meaning that an investor cannot borrow shares from a brokerage house or a bank and sell them in the market for an eventual gain. In the *urbun* arrangement, the trader who wishes to short a stock can put a sell order through the brokerage house, which then records the transaction as a purchase, not a loan. This process establishes ownership of the asset before sale to the market, and thus, the arrangement is *Shari'a* compliant. The mechanics of this structure are different from conventional shorting, but the economic effect is similar to that of a conventional short sale.

Despite the controversy, lack of standardization, and fledgling size of many capital market sectors characterizing the Islamic capital market today, the market is likely to continue to grow as the demand for Islamic investment products expands. The drivers of growth are a mixture of heightened investor awareness of the market, a broad range of products and their increasing availability, and increased interest in Islamic investing. Rising wealth levels in oil-rich nations also create a demand for investment products that can generate returns that are competitive with those of conventional, or Western, products.

Chapter 5. *Takaful*: Islamic Insurance

Islamic insurance, or *takaful*, has enjoyed remarkable growth in the past three decades in the Muslim community. Conventional, Western insurance is viewed by Islam as violating two of its primary tenets—the prohibitions against engaging in activities involving *gharar* (uncertainty) and *maisir* (gambling).[19]

In a conventional insurance system, the insured transfers the risk of loss or damage to an insurance company, which makes a profit if its premium and investment income exceed its incurred losses and underwriting expenses. In a *takaful* system, participants make payments to a common fund that is managed by a *takaful* operator under one of three models: *mudharabah* (profit sharing), *wakalah* (an agent who receives a management fee), or *wakalah* with *waqf* (a hybrid form of the *wakalah* model that uses a foundation, or *waqf*). The *takaful* operator does not assume the risk of loss or damage on the part of the participants. Rather, the risk is shared among the *takaful* participants whose contributions provide the means to cover any losses or damages incurred by themselves or others.

The first *takaful* company was established in 1979. As of 2006, more than 250 such companies operated around the world; in 2005, total premium income exceeded US$2.0 billion ("Takaful: A Market with Great Potential" 2006). The global *takaful* industry has recently been growing by an impressive 20 percent per year globally and at 25 percent per year in the GCC (Bhatty 2008). Moody's Investors Service predicts that global *takaful* premiums will reach US$7.0 billion by 2015. The Islamic insurance industry could be worth up to US$15 billion globally within next 10 years (Bowman 2008).

This chapter explains the *takaful* models, types of *takaful*, and the system's growth prospects. The focus is on the *takaful* industry in Malaysia, the current leader in the market.

Definition of *Takaful*

The word "*takaful*" is derived from the Arabic word "*kafalah*," which means "guaranteeing each other" or a "joint guarantee" and is based on the concept of social solidarity, cooperation, and mutual indemnification of losses. *Takaful* operates on the Islamic principles of *taawun* (brotherhood or mutual assistance) and *tabarru'* (donation, gift, or contribution). Thus, in *takaful*, the risk of loss is shared collectively and voluntarily by the participants, who guarantee each other against defined

---

[19]In 1985, the Islamic Fiqh Academy, a subsidiary of the Organization of the Islamic Conference, ruled that conventional commercial insurance is *haram* (forbidden) but that *takaful* is *halal* (permissible) because it is based on the application of shared responsibility, joint indemnity, common interest, and charitable donations.

losses or damages. Each participating member contributes resources (premium payments) and personal efforts to support the needy participants within the group. Consistent with Islamic beliefs, *takaful* is an example of how the fortunate may assist the unfortunate few.

The essence of *takaful* is to maintain equity among the members of a group and to assist those in the group who have suffered misfortune. Earning a profit is not the sole objective of the *takaful* operator or participants (who share in any surplus *takaful* funds). The *takaful* participant is viewed as both the insurer and the insured.

The following key elements must exist for a proper *takaful* system to be established:

- All *takaful* activities must be in compliance with *Shari'a*, which requires the presence of risk sharing based on the principles of *taawun* and *tabarru'*, coincidence of ownership, participation in management by policyholders, avoidance of *riba* (giving or receiving of interest) and prohibited investments, and inclusion of *mudharabah* and/or *wakalah* principles in management practices.
- *Takaful* participants must act with utmost sincerity (*neaa*) and adhere to the purpose and principles of *takaful*, which are cooperative and characterized by risk sharing and mutual assistance.
- All *takaful* dealings must be conducted in good faith and with honesty, transparency, truthfulness, and fairness, and all should be consistent with Islamic social and moral goals.
- All *takaful* activities must be free of *haram* (forbidden) elements.
- All *takaful* contracts must involve parties who have adequate legal knowledge and who are mentally competent.
- *Takaful* policies should be based on mutual consent and should specify a defined time period of policy coverage; the principle of indemnity must prevail.
- Oversight by a *Shari'a* advisory council must be provided because Islamic scholars have a role in defining what can be insured and also in approving the structure of final agreements.
- *Takaful* operations must undergo regular Islamic audits.

Precursors to *Takaful*

The foundations of *takaful* predate the rise of Islam. In the pre-Islamic era, the practice of *aquila* was common among ancient Arab tribes. *Aquila* was a mutual agreement or joint guarantee among Arab tribes to spread the financial liability should a member of one tribe kill or injure a member of another. When someone was killed, blood money, or *diyah*, was to be paid to the heirs of the victim by the paternal relatives of the accused. To mitigate the financial burden, the members of the accused tribe who were participants in the scheme would contribute until the *diyah* had been satisfied. Participating tribal members, therefore, collectively shared responsibility for sums individually owed.

Following the rise of Islam, Muslim Arab merchants who were expanding trade into Asia adopted the practice of *aquila*. They mutually agreed to contribute to a fund that would cover participants who incurred mishap or robbery during the numerous and dangerous sea voyages they undertook. The obligation to make regular financial payments to such a fund was similar to premiums paid for conventional insurance today. The compensation amount in the event of a mishap was similar to the indemnity or sum insured under modern insurance practices.

Today's *takaful* system incorporates many of the practices of its historical precedents.

Mudharabah Model of Takaful

Under the concept of *mudharabah* (profit sharing), the *takaful* participants (*rabb-ul-mal*) provide funds to the *takaful* operator (*mudarib*), who manages the funds and generates profits through *Shari'a*-compliant investments or trade. The parties to the *takaful* transaction enter into cooperative risk-sharing and profit-sharing agreements. The *takaful* operator shares in the profits earned from investments but not in the losses; the participants bear the sole burden of losses. The *mudharabah* model is depicted in **Figure 5.1**.

Figure 5.1. Simplified Form of *Takaful* Based on *Mudharabah* Model

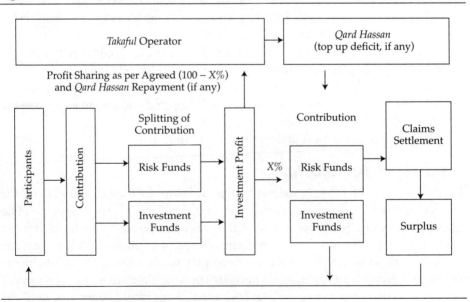

Sources: Kassim (2005) and Bank Negara Malaysia (2005).

Contributions are given on trust (*amanah*) to the *takaful* operator and, therefore, are repayable to the participants in due course minus the operator's costs. Contributions are split into two accounts—donations (*tabarru'*) and investment funds. These accounts must be clearly segregated to ensure that the participants are mutually insuring and bearing the risk of loss through their *tabarru'*.

Tabarru' Contribution. The *tabarru'* contribution, or risk fund contribution, is a donation dedicated to the compensation of *takaful* participants who experience losses or damages. The *takaful* participant agrees to relinquish as *tabarru'* a certain percentage of the total *takaful* contribution or premium. The *tabarru'* contribution fulfills the participant's obligation of mutual help and joint guarantee that is necessary in accordance with *Shari'a*.

Investment Fund Contribution. The investment fund contribution is the amount remaining after the total *takaful* contribution is reduced by the percentage designated as *tabarru'*. The *takaful* operator invests the funds in *Shari'a*-compliant investments for the purpose of generating profits. The investment profits are distributed, under the principle of *mudharabah*, among the participants and the operator on the basis of a predetermined percentage. All investment losses are borne entirely by the *takaful* participants; the *takaful* operator does not participate.

Tabarru' Surplus. The funds remaining in the *tabarru'* account after all claims and related expenses have been paid are considered the surplus or, if the amount is negative, the deficit. The surplus or deficit is shared collectively on the basis of a predetermined ratio among the participants (the operator is included in certain countries) at maturity of the policy. In the event of a loss in the *tabarru'* fund, the *takaful* operator typically offers participants financing to fund their portion of the loss on the basis of the principle of *qard hassan* (a benevolent, or profit-free, loan). The *qard hassan* loan has to be repaid when the *tabarru'* fund returns to profitability and prior to the distribution of any future *tabarru'* surplus.

Wakalah Model of *Takaful*

In the *wakalah* model (the word "*wakalah*" is Arabic for "delegation" or "representation"), a contract provides that the *takaful* operator will manage the *takaful* fund on behalf of the participants and will be compensated by a fee called a *wakalah* fee. In effect, the operator is appointed as an agent (*wakalah*), and a fee (*ujr*) is paid for this agent's expertise. The fee may be a percentage of the *takaful* contribution (premium) or an absolute amount. **Figure 5.2** illustrates the simplified form of the *wakalah* model of *takaful*.

The *wakalah* model is gaining in popularity because of increasing objections to the practice of sharing the surplus funds with the *takaful* operator, as is provided for in the *mudharabah* model. In the *wakalah* model, the *takaful* operator acts as agent and does not share in any surplus funds earned from investing. The *wakalah*

Figure 5.2. Simplified Form of *Wakalah* Model of *Takaful*

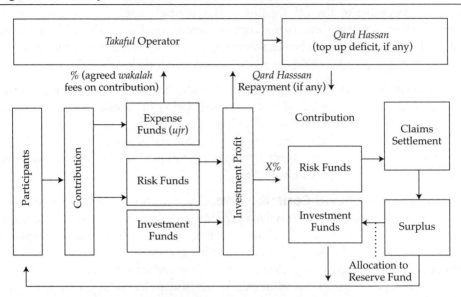

Sources: Kassim (2005) and Bank Negara Malaysia (2005).

model of *takaful* is currently offered in 30 countries. The *wakalah* model is preferred also because it is regarded as providing better insurance protection than the *mudharabah* model, which is considered more friendly to the investment manager.

Tabarru' Contribution. As in the *mudharabah* model, a percentage of the total *takaful* contribution is segregated as *tabarru'*. The *tabarru'* contribution is further split into a risk fund and an investment fund. The rationale for having two funds is the same as in the *mudharabah* model. The risk fund is used to pay claims; it is treated as a donation to help the needy (participants who experience losses or damages) and to fulfill the *Shari'a* requirement of mutual risk sharing. The investment funds are invested in *Shari'a*-compliant investments.

Expense Fund Contribution. The *ujr* equals the difference between the total *takaful* contribution, or premium, and the amount of the *tabarru'* contribution. The *ujr* funds are segregated in the expense fund.

Tabarru' Surplus. Any surplus funds that are generated from the *tabarru'* funds may be used in one of three ways. First, the entire surplus may be kept in the *tabarru'* fund. Second, a certain portion may be kept in the fund as a contingency reserve, and the balance may be distributed to the participants. Third, after making provisions for a contingency reserve, the balance may be distributed among the participants and the *takaful* operator. The method by which surplus funds will be distributed is disclosed to participants prior to their participation in the plan.

As in the *mudharabah* model, any losses in the *tabarru'*, or risk, fund are borne by the participants. The *takaful* operator typically extends financing on the basis of the *qard hassan* (benevolent loan) principle. The loans must be repaid by participants before any future surplus is distributed to them.

Wakalah-with-*Waqf* Model of *Takaful*

The *wakalah*-with-*waqf* model is a refinement of the *wakalah* model and incorporates a separate legal entity known as a *waqf* to hold shareholder donations and participant contributions. A *waqf* is essentially a gift of land or property intended for religious, educational, or charitable purposes, and the use of a *waqf* is an accepted practice in most Muslim countries. The *waqf* is a *Shari'a*-compliant entity that can operate under direct ownership of the *waqf* assets or, alternatively, with a third party that owns the assets. Unlike in the *mudharabah* and *wakalah* models, the participants do not own the *takaful* or *waqf* funds. **Figure 5.3** shows the simplified form of the *wakalah*-with-*waqf* model.

The *waqf* funds are managed on a fee basis by an appointed fund manager or administrator. The *takaful* operator, or *mudarib*, has its own shareholders and, in addition to receiving a fee to manage the *waqf* assets and to administer the *takaful* plan, shares in any profit from the *waqf*'s investments, which are funded by both shareholder donations and participant contributions. The profit or loss of the *takaful* operator is passed on to its shareholders.

Figure 5.3.   Simplified *Wakalah*-with-*Waqf* Model of *Takaful*

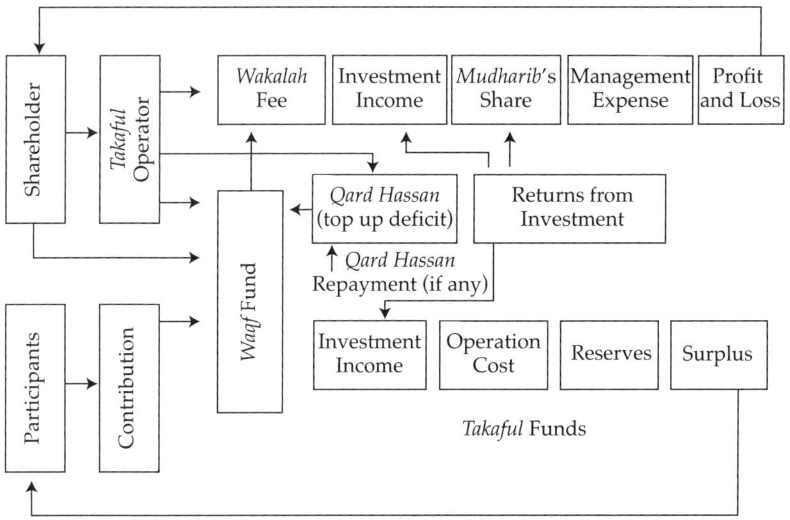

Source: Adapted from Pirani (2007).

Shareholder Donations. Shareholders of the *takaful* operator's company, who may also be *takaful* participants, make a donation (the amount may be specified by Islamic scholars) to establish the *waqf* fund. The shareholders have no ownership rights in the *waqf*, but they do have the right to administer the *waqf* funds and to develop the rules and regulations that govern it. The *waqf* funds are invested in *Shari'a*-compliant products, and the returns are used for the benefit of *takaful* participants. There is no obligation to distribute any surplus *waqf* funds to the shareholders.

Participant Contributions. The *tabarru'* contributions made by the participants are also deposited in the *waqf*. The *waqf* funds, after the *takaful* operator's fees to cover management, administration, and marketing expenses are deducted, are invested in *Shari'a*-compliant products. Any claims from participants to cover losses or damages are paid from the *waqf*. In addition, all operational costs, such as re-*takaful* (similar to re-insurance in the conventional insurance model) or the building up of reserves, are met from the *waqf*.

Surplus Funds Distribution. The rules of the *waqf* define the basis for compensation to participants for losses suffered and may also provide for the manner in which any surplus funds are to be shared, but no obligation exists to distribute surplus funds to *takaful* participants.

As in the case of the *mudharabah* and *wakalah* models, the *takaful* operator covers any losses in the *waqf* through a *qard hassan* (benevolent) loan. This loan is made to the *waqf* entity, however, not to individual participants. Such loans must be repaid by participant contributions before any future surplus funds can be distributed.

Types of *Takaful*

Takaful plans can be divided into family *takaful* plans and general *takaful* plans.

Family *Takaful* Plans. A family *takaful* plan has three basic forms: the individual *takaful* plan, a mortgage *takaful* plan, and a health/medical *takaful* plan.

The individual *takaful* plan is a long-term savings and investment program with a fixed maturity period. It is similar in purpose to a term life insurance plan in the conventional insurance system but is entirely different in terms of mechanism and transaction structure. Its aims are

1. to encourage people to save regularly,
2. to earn and share profits from investing in *Shari'a*-compliant products, and
3. to pay *takaful* benefits to any heir(s) should a participant die before the maturity date of his or her *takaful* plan or to the participant in the case of disability.

If a participant dies before the end of the plan's terms, the participant's family members are entitled to the following benefits:

- the total contribution paid to date—that is, up to the due date of the installment payment just prior to the participant's death—plus the participant's share of the profits earned from investments credited to the account and
- the participant's remaining *takaful* installments under the term of the plan calculated from the date of death (these benefits are paid from the *tabarru'* fund).

If a participant outlives the *takaful*'s term, the following benefits are paid to the participant:

- the total amount of contributions paid by the participant plus the share of profits earned from investments credited to the participant's account and
- any surplus *tabarru'* funds allocated to the participant's account.

Should the participant be compelled to surrender or withdraw from the *takaful* plan before the maturity of the plan, the participant is entitled to receive the proportion of *takaful* installments that have been credited to the account plus the participant's share of investment profits. The amount that has been relinquished as *tabarru'*, however, is not refunded.

Mortgage *takaful* is a family *takaful* plan that automatically settles the policyholder's house financing in the event of his or her death or permanent disability. In most cases, the policyholder needs to pay only a single contribution for the mortgage *takaful*. The contribution rate depends on the policyholder's age, the amount of protection bought, the profit rate, and the amount of time for which the protection is valid. If the policyholder sells the house or redeems the financing earlier than the term, the policyholder is entitled to receive a pro rata refund of the contribution for the unexpired period of *takaful* ("Home Takaful" 2007).

Health or medical *takaful* covers the cost of private medical treatment, such as the cost of hospitalization and a doctor's care, if the policyholder is diagnosed with certain illnesses or has an accident. The coverage could be on a stand-alone basis or could act as a supplementary contract to a basic family *takaful* plan ("Medical & Health Takaful" 2007).

General *Takaful*. General *takaful* schemes are basically joint-guarantee contracts that provide compensation to participants in the event of a defined loss. They are short term in nature (normally one year), cover individuals or commercial entities, and insure real and personal property. The types of general *takaful* schemes offered include fire *takaful*, motor (automobile) *takaful*, and marine *takaful*.

History of *Takaful* in Malaysia

Malaysia, with a penetration rate of about 30 percent compared with about 5 percent in other Muslim countries, is ahead of most Muslim countries in developing the *takaful* market. Malaysia's *takaful* industry began in 1985 when the country's first *takaful* operator, Syarikat Takaful Malaysia, opened for business. This development followed the establishment in 1982 of a special task force to study the possibility of establishing Islamic insurance in the country.

The second *takaful* operator, MNI (Malaysia National Insurance) Takaful, opened its doors in 1994. Renamed Takaful Nasional in 1998, it is a subsidiary of a Malaysian conventional insurer. In 1997, a full-fledged re-*takaful* company, ASEAN Retakaful International, was incorporated in Malaysia's offshore financial center, Labuan, to support the re-*takaful* needs of the region's *takaful* operators. Its shareholders are *takaful* operators based in Malaysia, Brunei, and Singapore. In 2008, the country had eight *takaful* operators, twice the number in 2003.

At year-end 2007, total *takaful* contributions in Malaysia had risen 48.6 percent year-over-year to 2.6 billion Malaysian ringgits (RM), or US$845 million. At year-end 2003, total *takaful* contributions in Malaysia stood at RM1.0 billion, or US$264 million. And at year-end 2007, total *takaful* fund assets in Malaysia had climbed 18.6 percent year-over-year to RM8.8 billion, or US$2.65 billion, and accounted for 7.2 percent of total Malaysian insurance company assets. Approximately 85 percent of *takaful* assets were held in family *takaful* plans, with the remaining assets in general *takaful* plans. In 2003, total *takaful* fund assets were RM4.4 billion, or US$1.16 billion—that is, 5.6 percent of the total Malaysian insurance industry's assets (Ernst & Young 2007).

Malaysia actively promotes *takaful* products, especially family *takaful* plans, as a tool to increase savings within the Muslim community and as an essential component in ensuring economic growth and accelerating the investment potential of the *ummah*—the Muslim community as a whole.

Prospects for Global *Takaful* Growth

Takaful market growth is forecasted to increase substantially over the next decade. Moody's Investors Service projects global *takaful* premiums to rise to US$7.4 billion in 2015; Ernst & Young estimates that global *takaful* premiums will reach US$4.3 billion in 2010 if Iran is excluded and reach almost US$15 billion if Iran is included (Ernst & Young 2007).

The greatest prospects for growth in the *takaful* market are in the countries of the Middle East, which have historically had a low level of insurance penetration—conventional or *takaful* (Ernst & Young 2007).

Figure 5.4 compares the prospects for *takaful* by 2015 in various countries as projected by premium revenues in U.S. dollars. Malaysia is expected to continue to dominate the market, but Indonesia is expected to follow closely on its heels, with Saudi Arabia, the United States, and Iran rounding out the top five nations in terms of projected *takaful* premium revenues in 2015.

Figure 5.4. Potential for *Takaful* by Year 2015 for Selected Countries

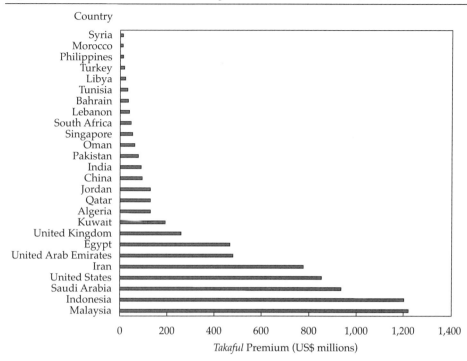

Source: Reorient Legal (no date).

The following factors point to the potential for growth in the *takaful* market over the next five years:

- The global trend of a Muslim preference for Islamic financial products, including *takaful*, will continue.
- Banca*takaful* (*Shari'a*-compliant bancassurance) offers a venue for *takaful* to expand by tapping into a bank's infrastructure and marketing mechanism.[20]
- Support by regulators, such as Bank Negara Malaysia, the Islamic Financial Services Board, and the Accounting and Auditing Organization for Islamic Financial Institutions, is facilitating the development of all Islamic financial products, including *takaful*.
- A broad range of products is needed to stimulate new demand as conventional insurers enter the market.

---

[20]Bancassurance (a term for the Bank Insurance Model) is the term used to describe the partnership or relationship between a bank and an insurance company whereby the insurance company uses the financial institution's sales channels to sell insurance products.

- Global insurance giants, such as Prudential and Allianz, are raising awareness of the Islamic insurance industry through their significant brand recognition.
- An active marketing appeal to non-Muslims is being undertaken. In Malaysia, non-Muslims account for around 35 percent of the *takaful* customer base; in Sri Lanka, some 15 percent of *takaful* policyholders are non-Muslims.
- There is a shift in perception toward the idea that *takaful* is both an investment solution and an insurance product.

Challenges for the *Takaful* Industry

Although growth in the *takaful* industry has been strong in certain countries and the prospects for broader, more sustained growth are positive, the *takaful* industry still faces a number of challenges.

First, because *takaful* is a fairly young industry, corporate governance policies for *takaful* operators are still developing. Regulatory bodies must step in to implement appropriate policies and standards to ensure *Shari'a* compliance and to avoid conflicts between the operators, shareholders, and policyholders.

Second, a greater number of well-known, established credit-rating agencies need to rate *takaful* companies regarding their *Shari'a* compliance, financial strength, and solvency to strengthen consumer confidence in them. Currently, only the Islamic International Rating Agency and Moody's offer such ratings.

Third, consumers need more information about the benefits and mechanics of *takaful*. The three *takaful* business models—*mudharabah*, *wakalah*, and *wakalah* with *waqf*—create confusion among consumers and doubt about *Shari'a* compliance.

Fourth, more *takaful* products are needed that are competitive with conventional insurance products, particularly in meeting the needs of commercial customers. More investment needs to be made in cost-effective technology and methods to take advantage of new distribution channels, such as the internet and banca*takaful*, to reach more customers.

Fifth, a shortage of skilled *takaful* staff exists.

Sixth, the pace has been slow in solving a combination of technical, legal, tax, *Shari'a*, and accounting issues in certain Muslim countries, such as Indonesia, which has hampered the entry of international *takaful* players into potentially strong markets.

Chapter 6. Islam and Private Wealth Management

The Islamic wealth management (IWM) industry is the fastest growing segment of Islamic finance. The segment represents an estimated US$1.3 trillion of personal Muslim wealth in the Gulf Cooperation Council (GCC) countries alone.[21] In addition, significant wealth is being created in India, Malaysia, and Indonesia.

The growth of the IWM sector of financial services has been fueled by rising personal wealth in the Middle East and Southeast Asia as oil prices have dramatically risen, coupled with strengthening demand for *Shari'a*-compliant wealth generation products as Muslims seek to identify with the teachings of Islam. In addition to unprecedented oil-related wealth creation, wealth has multiplied in the Muslim community because of widespread robust macroeconomic growth in emerging Asian nations, diversification in business and financial investment in the Middle East, and new foreign direct investment in Southeast Asia driven by rising commodity prices (Lim 2008; KFH Research 2008).

The scope of IWM, as in conventional private wealth management or private banking, is much wider than simply investment management. It encompasses liability and risk management as well as inheritance and tax planning for high-net-worth (HNW) individuals. Practically speaking, however, other than overlaying Islamic principles on investment selection and obeying religious restrictions on wealth transfer in a decedent's estate, Islamic private banking essentially shares the same goals and practices as conventional private banking.

This chapter focuses on the Islamic definition of wealth, the Islamic wealth creation and management cycle, Islamic inheritance law, the size of and prospects for this market sector, and the drivers of and challenges to the continued growth of global Islamic wealth and Islamic wealth management.

Wealth and Islam

Islam teaches that wealth can be obtained through effort or through inheritance but that all wealth (*maal*) belongs to Allah and that mankind is only a trustee of this wealth. In Islam, wasting wealth is scorned. Money should be earned, invested, and spent in approved (*halal*) ways—that is, in compliance with Islamic principles. Only in this way will a Muslim, his or her family, and society (*ummah*) obtain rewards in this life and also hereafter (Salim 2006).

---

[21]The GCC consists of Bahrain, Kuwait, Oman, Qatar, Saudi Arabia, and the United Arab Emirates. See Nambiar (2008).

Islam does not discourage the acquisition of wealth, but it maintains that obsessive preoccupation in accumulating and building wealth by an individual leads to the sidelining of the most essential part of the self—one's spirituality. The same is considered true for a government or a society. And although Islam does not view the accumulation of wealth negatively, it does frown on excessive accumulation of wealth in the hands of a few. The *zakat* tax system, which effectively redistributes wealth from the "haves" to the "have-nots," is one of the five pillars of Islam. Inheritance rules also ensure that wealth is evenly shared among the *ummah*.

Islam requires that Muslims seek to acquire enduring *and endearing* wealth. For this purpose, Islam encourages Muslims to work and earn a legitimate income for themselves and their families and implores every Muslim to work hard to achieve perfection and excellence in his or her chosen profession. Thus, the practices of Islamic wealth management incorporate the creation, enhancement, protection, distribution, and purification of wealth.

The Islamic Perspective on Wealth Creation, Management, and Distribution

Shari'a teaches that wealth serves many purposes and should neither be expended on unlawful products and services nor spent in vain or ostentatiously. According to *Shari'a*, the need to attain wealth provides the motivation to work hard. The ability of a person to create and to equitably distribute wealth gives hope to the poor and needy, and the need to manage wealth provides the discipline to save in order to support family and society. By saving even a small portion of income or profits and eschewing wasteful spending, a Muslim can help fight consumerism and inflation (Salim 2006). **Figure 6.1** portrays the cycle of wealth creation, enhancement, protection, and distribution with which all private banking functions, conventional and Islamic, are concerned.

Wealth Creation. In Islam, Allah owns the wealth and bestows it on mankind. Allah is the absolute owner of wealth; mankind is the trustee of wealth. Wealth should be earned and multiplied in an Islamically permissible way, which means income and capital appreciation must not be generated from prohibited business activities.

Wealth Enhancement. Enhancement of wealth in Islam is achieved through investing only in *Shari'a*-complaint financial products—that is, products entirely free from *riba* (usury) and largely free of *gharar* (uncertainty) and *maisir* (gambling); moreover, the investing must not involve *haram* (forbidden) products, such as pork and alcohol. Such financial products include stocks, investment funds, bonds (*sukuk*), insurance (*takaful*) plans, *wadiah* and *mudharabah* savings plans, and the funding of new investment through *Shari'a*-compliant financing arrangements. The goal of IWM, which is similar to the goal of conventional wealth management, is to garner reasonable capital growth while preserving accumulated wealth.

Figure 6.1. Cycle of Wealth Creation, Enhancement, Protection, and Distribution

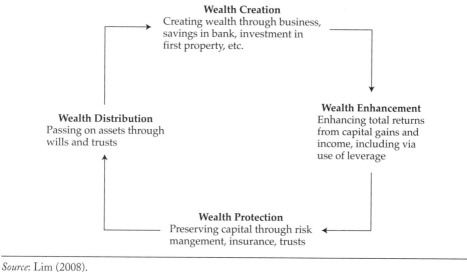

Wealth Creation
Creating wealth through business, savings in bank, investment in first property, etc.

Wealth Enhancement
Enhancing total returns from capital gains and income, including via use of leverage

Wealth Distribution
Passing on assets through wills and trusts

Wealth Protection
Preserving capital through risk mangement, insurance, trusts

Source: Lim (2008).

Wealth Protection. The protection of wealth is crucial according to Islam; every conceivable financial risk and threat must be considered and provided for. Therefore, risk management and Islamic insurance (*takaful*) play an important role in the practice of IWM. And investing in *Shari'a*-compliant financial products that are viewed as being structured to avoid *gharar* is consistent with the Islamic admonishment to protect wealth.

Wealth Cleansing and Distribution. Islam requires both physical and spiritual cleanliness. Cleanliness of the spirit involves cleanliness of the mind, so that it is free of bad intent or desire to commit unlawful acts, and cleanliness of the heart, so that it is free from jealousy, hypocrisy, and evil desires. Spiritual cleanliness is associated with hope, truthfulness, forgiveness, and compassion. To aid Muslims in achieving spiritual cleanliness and wealth purification, Islam espouses the *zakat* tax system. It is mandatory for every Muslim whose wealth has reached a certain level to pay *zakat*, which is fixed at a rate equivalent to 2.5 percent of a person's or household's financial assets or tradable goods. *Zakat* is a means of narrowing the gap between rich and poor and a way to help meet the needs of less fortunate members of society.

Wealth distribution also takes place through the inheritance law, or *faraid*, which governs the distribution of the estate of a Muslim after death.

Faraid

Faraid, or the Islamic law of inheritance, automatically includes the spouse, parents, and children (known as Quranic heirs) of the decedent as the heirs to the decedent's estate. Grandchildren, adopted children, illegitimate children, foster parents, non-Muslim parents, non-Muslim children, and non-Muslim family members are not automatically included as heirs under Islamic law. A Muslim may dispose of one-third of his or her estate as he/she wishes. Therefore, up to one-third of a decedent's estate may be bequeathed among non-*Shari'a* heirs through the provisions of a will. A will (*wasiyat*) is considered to be a religious obligation of all Muslims, but it may be either oral or written. Normally, the will must be declared in the presence of two witnesses in order to be valid, but an exception exists, according to the Islamic schools of Maliki and Hanbali—namely, a will is still acceptable if it is written in the known handwriting of the testator or bears his or her known signature.

The size of the estate is determined after payment of funeral expenses and debts and the discharging of spousal rights to mutually acquired properties, incomplete lifetime gifts (*hibah*) and after-death legacies to nonheirs (made via the *wasiyat*). The majority view is that debts to Allah, such as *zakat*, should be paid regardless of their mention in the will, although this view is a matter of debate among Muslim jurists (Hussain, no date).

The differences between Muslim and non-Muslim wills are enumerated in Exhibit 6.1.

Exhibit 6.1. Differences between Islamic and Non-Islamic Wills

Islamic Will	Non-Islamic Will
Islamic law determines the disposition of the majority of a decedent's assets.	The disposition of all the decedent's assets is determined by the decedent.
Distribution of a decedent's estate to Quranic heirs (spouse, children, and parents) is provided for under the inheritance law. No changes can be made to this predetermined distribution by a decedent's will.	A decedent has full discretion in determining the distribution of the estate to spouse, children, parents, and any other heirs specified.
Only one-third of a decedent's estate can be distributed to non-Quranic heirs without the consent of the Quranic heirs.	A decedent may determine the disposition of 100 percent of his or her estate.

Zakat

Paying *zakat* is considered to be a form of worshipping Allah. The original meaning of the word *zakat* is both "purification" and "growth." Paying *zakat* is an obligation for Muslims to fulfill. It is the third of the five pillars of Islam, and its importance is no different from that of the other obligations.[22] Giving *zakat* means "giving a

---

[22]The other pillars of Islam are faith, prayers, fasting, and *hajji* (or pilgrimage).

specified percentage of certain assets to certain classes of needy people." Muslims believe that payment of *zakat* leads to cleansing the heart from evil. There are two main types of *zakat*:

- *Zakat fitr* is due from the start of Ramadan until the prayer ending Ramadan (*eid al-fitr*). Every Muslim except those living in absolute poverty must contribute a certain amount of staple foods or the equivalent in money.
- *Zakat* on *maal*: This type of *zakat* is payable on traditional types of wealth, such as agricultural produce, reared animals, a business, gold, and silver.

The belief is that wealth is a gift from Allah; if able, one has the duty to use part of it to help one's needy brethren. This redistribution of wealth is a way to reduce social inequality.

Prospects for Islamic Wealth Management

The report "Tapping Global High Net Worth Individuals" (KFH Research 2008) states that more and more Muslim HNW individuals are turning to Islamic wealth management. Many are strongly committed to using financial services that are fully compatible with *Shari'a* principles and are shunning investments in industries viewed as unethical, such as alcohol or gambling. Increased financial transparency and disclosure and regular monitoring for compliance by the relevant *Shari'a* boards have also encouraged demand. In general, acceptance of Islamic financial services and products, such as *sukuk*, private equity, and structured products, has been growing.

In 2008, Muslim private wealth is estimated to have represented some 5 percent (US$2.1 trillion) of global private wealth, up from an estimated 4.8 percent (US$1.9 trillion) in 2007. And Muslim private wealth is projected to rise by 2020 to an estimated US$4 trillion as the world's Muslim population increases to an estimated 2.5 billion, up from the current estimate of 1.5 billion (KFH Research 2008).

Although growth of the Islamic wealth management sector has been strong, IWM faces the same challenges that Islamic finance, in general, faces if it is to expand to its full potential. A major hurdle for future growth of the industry is a skills shortage. The number of religious scholars with sufficient credentials to issue rulings on new products is limited, as is the number of well-trained lawyers, bankers, and technical staff who are needed to implement contracts and develop new products. An Islamic scholar must train for about 15 years in Islamic jurisprudence and finance. Players in the industry often lack the necessary information, and academic research and market data are often incomplete and inconsistent.

In addition to skilled and educated human capital, for IWM to advance, it needs a higher level of standardization in investment products and consistency in the application of screening criteria for *Shari'a* compliance. Often, no single interpretation of Islamic law prevails throughout a particular jurisdiction, so each financial institution in that jurisdiction has its own board of religious scholars to determine which products are *halal* (permissible) under Islam.

Affluent and HNW Islamic investors are becoming markedly more sophisticated and adventurous in their financial demands than in the past, however, and are turning to hedge funds and other complex capital market products to earn a competitive return. Although the religious credentialing of financial products is important to these investors, the potential for return may be the deciding factor. A common position taken by private and institutional investors is that they prefer to invest in Islamic funds when possible, so long as they do not have to sacrifice return to do so.

Chapter 7. Corporate Governance for Islamic Financial Institutions

For Islamic financial institutions, the adoption of best practices for corporate governance is crucial for competing effectively on the world stage and to preserve the institutions' reputations. Sound corporate governance—for Islamic and conventional enterprises—is an imperative for long-term success. By fostering a culture based on ethics and accountability, strong governance policies and practices serve to enhance corporate value and support stakeholder interests.

Good corporate governance is needed to address the opaqueness inherent in the management of financial institutions. Particularly for an outsider (potential and existing customers and investors), assessing investment performance, the performance or profitability of the institution itself, the risks taken, and the presence of outright ethical or legal violations is hard. Therefore, regulatory bodies play an important role as watchdogs for both conventional and Islamic banks. Because of their profit-and-loss–sharing model and newness on the scene, however, Islamic banks pose special corporate governance challenges, especially with regard to the rights of investment account holders and in the setting up of a *Shari'a* supervisory board to ensure compliance with *Shari'a* principles.

Corporate Governance

The term "corporate governance" refers to the way an organization is directed, administered, or controlled. It includes the set of policies and practices that affect managers' decision making and contribute to the way a company is perceived by current and potential stakeholders. Good corporate governance procedures ensure that the management team is held properly accountable and promote personal integrity, strong internal controls, and appropriate risk management practices at the institution.

Corporate governance generally has two components: self-governance and statutory regulation. Self-governance relates to areas that are difficult to legislate, such as leadership transition, independence of the board of directors, appraisal of directors' performance, and directors' relationships with managers (Nordin 2002). Statutory regulation encompasses the rules and regulations of governing authorities that companies must comply with. Regulatory statutes typically cover the duties, obligations, rights, and liabilities of directors, controlling shareholders, and company officers. They also generally apply to the timeliness and quality of corporate disclosures, as well as accounting standards and practices.

Corporate Governance in Islam

The Islamic concept of corporate governance emphasizes the traits that Allah (God) expects in people: accountability, transparency, and trustworthiness (Mustapha and Salleh 2002). Thus, according to Islam, a company's managers and staff, by virtue of their individual responsibility to religious principles, are accountable to the shareholders, customers, regulatory bodies, and society at large. In Islam, self-governance is encouraged by the principle of *tawhid*, which promotes the need to submit fully to God. *Tawhid* focuses on the unique relationship between people and Allah and seeks to prevent people from behaving in a harmful way toward all living creatures. Acting responsibly toward others and being responsible for oneself is an *amanah* (literally, trust), or act of the free will given by God. Neglecting personal and social responsibilities is a form of *khianat* (betrayal) in the eyes of God. Muslims are also called to be dedicated to their work. Work and dedication to work are a form of *ibadah* (worship) and are viewed as an *amal salih* (virtuous act). Acting with integrity is required of a practicing Muslim under the principle of *khilafah* (trustee-ship). All of these aspects of Islam support the goal of strong corporate governance.

Shari'a governs Islamic financial institutions just as it governs individuals and their actions. The aim of *Shari'a* for financial institutions is to support Islamic financial practices that do not exploit or do injustice to the institution's shareholders and customers. Three basic elements of the Islamic faith provide the foundation for corporate governance in Islamic banking (Haron and Shanmugam 1997): (1) *aqidah*, which concerns all forms of faith and belief in Allah, (2) *Shari'a*, the law, which concerns practical actions taken by Muslims in manifesting their faith and beliefs, and (3) *akhlaq*, which covers all aspects of a Muslim's behavior, attitude, and work ethic (see Chapter 2 for more information about these concepts). Islam inculcates into the faithful the principles necessary for strong corporate governance by providing spiritual backing to these tenets, which enforces their adoption among believers.

In fact, some Islamic scholars have argued that strict adherence to Islamic religious principles is sufficient to counter the problems of conflicts of interest in incentive that are inherent in financial institutions, such as an institution's *ex post* determination of the client's share of profits and an institution's unilateral decision-making ability in investing client funds. The argument is that the Islamic moral code will prevent Muslims from behaving in ways that are ethically unsound and that Islamic religious ideology acts as its own incentive mechanism to reduce the inefficiency that arises from asymmetric information and moral hazard (Suleiman 2005). Prudent managers of financial institutions, however, do not depend on the individual's relationship with his or her God to ensure compliance with legal and ethical obligations; additional measures should be taken.

Corporate Governance Framework in Islamic Financial Institutions

An Islamic corporate governance framework has been developed by regulatory bodies and/or central banks in various countries to facilitate good governance practices and end poor governance practices at Islamic financial institutions. The important components of the framework are illustrated in **Figure 7.1**. The framework provides standards and guidelines that are in accordance with *Shari'a*; addresses the intermediary and multifaceted roles of Islamic financial institutions; seeks to ensure accountability, transparency, and an adequate division of power among stakeholders; and seeks to avoid conflicts of interest.

Figure 7.1.   Responsible Parties for Implementation of Corporate Governance

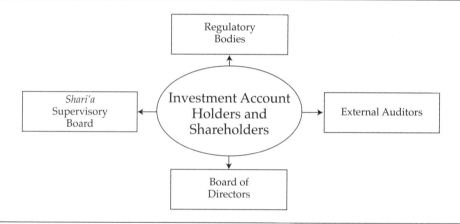

Islamic banks operate on the principle of profit-and-loss sharing. Thus, the funds contributed by investment account holders are more than mere deposits; they are, in part, equity investments. Investment account holders lack some of the rights that a shareholder enjoys, however, even though, like shareholders, they are a type of equityholder with residual claims to their share of the bank's assets (Archer, Abdel Karim, and Al-Deehani 1998).

Hence, an Islamic corporate governance framework should encompass the interests of all stakeholders, including the fair treatment of minority shareholders and investment account holders at Islamic banks, as is encouraged in the Islamic faith under the concept of *taqwa* (righteousness). The governance framework should also encourage transparency and disclosure regarding decision making in all areas of an institution's professional competence, which is of paramount importance to investment account holders because their funds are normally pooled together with those of shareholders. The framework prescribes disclosure rules, firewalls to protect against conflicts of interest, and sanctions for breaches.

The governance structures of Islamic financial institutions are distinguished from conventional governance structures by the addition of a *Shari'a* advisory body. Usually, each Islamic financial institution has its own in-house religious advisers who compose the *Shari'a* supervisory or advisory board and whose responsibility is to ensure that the institution's business practices and products conform to Islamic law. The existence of the advisory board mitigates the institution's exposure to fiduciary and reputational risks related to Islamic standards of compliance, which, in turn, boosts the confidence of Muslim shareholders and the *ummah* (Muslim community) in the institution.

Islamic corporate governance practices may require the composition of the *Shari'a* advisory body to be disclosed and all *fatwa* (religious opinions) issued by the advisory body to be published. Such public disclosures strengthen stakeholders' confidence in the credibility of the institution's assessment of its *Shari'a* compliance. The roles of various parties in the corporate governance framework as practiced in Malaysia are illustrated in **Exhibit 7.1.**

To provide sufficient oversight and to protect the interests of the investment account holders, the Malaysia-based Islamic Financial Services Board (IFSB), which issues standards and guiding principles for the Islamic financial industry, has advocated the creation of a special corporate governance committee at each institution. The IFSB has stated that the committee should be established by an institution's board of directors and that it should comprise three members: a nonexecutive director selected on the basis of experience and ability, an audit committee member, and a *Shari'a* scholar, who may be a member of the company's *Shari'a* supervisory board.

Exhibit 7.1. Illustration of Roles of Elements in a Corporate Governance Framework

Body	Tasks	Reports
SC and BNM SAC	Promulgate national *Shari'a* rulings, opinions, and policies	*Shari'a* rulings and basis; approved products and services
SC and BNM supervisory review	Conduct supervision of IFI *Shari'a* opinions and policies	Specific guidelines and reports on *Shari'a* compliance
Shari'a supervisory boards and *Shari'a* committees	Formulate and review financial institution's *Shari'a* opinions and policies	Comprehensive *Shari'a* supervisory report
External auditors	Undertake financial audit to express true and fair opinion	External audit report
Boards of directors; audit and governance committees	Structure internal control processes and activities of an institution to be *Shari'a* compliant	Statement of corporate governance

Note: SC = Securities Commission Malaysia; BNM SAC = Bank Negara Malaysia *Shari'a* Advisory Council; IFI = Islamic Financial Institution.

Source: Alhabshi 2007.

To summarize, because investment account holders and shareholders of the same institution are exposed to similar risks—through the principle of *mudharabah* (risk sharing)—but investment account holders do not always receive proportionate rewards for those risks, special care must be taken to protect the interests of investment account holders (see Chapter 3 for more information on the mechanics of Islamic investment accounts).

Figure 7.2 depicts the recommended governance structure for a typical Islamic financial institution.

Figure 7.2. Governance Structure for an Islamic Financial Institution

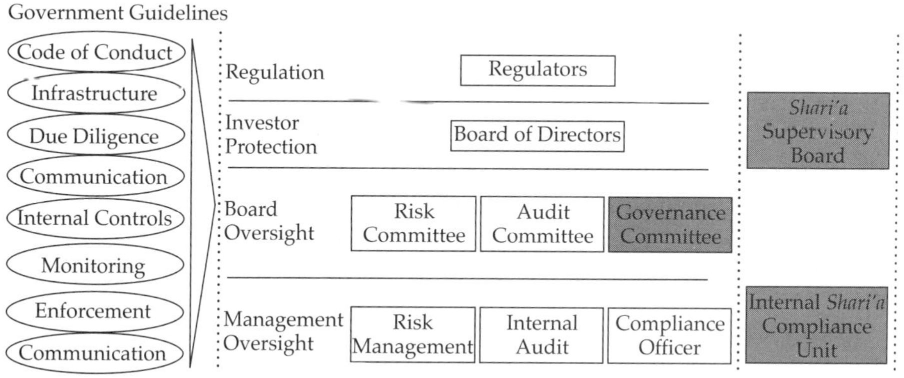

Source: Stanley (2008).

Islamic Corporate Governance Models in Various Countries

In this section, we compare the corporate governance models for Islamic financial institutions in Malaysia, Pakistan, Kuwait, Bahrain, the United Arab Emirates, and Qatar.

Malaysia. Bank Negara Malaysia (BNM), the Malaysian central bank, monitors and supervises Islamic financial institutions in Malaysia (also refer to Exhibit 7.1). Financial institutions are governed by the Islamic Banking Act 1983, which stipulates that a financial institution must have an internal *Shari'a* supervisory board consisting of three to seven Muslim religious scholars. BNM has also issued "Guidelines on the Governance of *Shari'a* Committees for Islamic Financial Institutions."

BNM established the national *Shari'a* Advisory Council (SAC) under Section 16B of the Central Bank of Malaysia Act 1958. The work of the council and the *Shari'a* committees of individual financial institutions are complementary, as shown in **Exhibit 7.2**. The SAC arbitrates disputes and is the final authority on all matters

Exhibit 7.2. Malaysia Model: *Shari'a* Advisory Council and *Shari'a* Committees at Islamic Financial Institution

Shari'a Advisory Council	*Shari'a* Committee at Islamic Financial Institution
• Independent central *Shari'a* council commands public confidence. • *Shari'a* council promotes harmonization and uniformity of *Shari'a* interpretations. • Council is the highest authority on *Shari'a* matters and a reference point for court decisions.	• *Shari'a* committee provides checks and balances to ensure *Shari'a* compliance. • Committee advises Islamic financial institution on *Shari'a* matters. • Committee endorses *Shari'a* compliance manuals and product documentations. • Committee assists in internal audit of Islamic financial institution as to *Shari'a* compliance.

Source: Ibrahim (2007).

pertaining to Islamic finance in Malaysia, including *takaful* (Islamic insurance). (Remember that Islamic banking and *takaful* are considered separate industries.) Its resolutions are binding, and when a *Shari'a*-related dispute is under the jurisdiction of the Malaysian legal system, the SAC advises the court.

Members of the national *Shari'a* Advisory Council cannot serve on the *Shari'a* committee of a financial institution, and each *Shari'a* scholar can serve as a *Shari'a* committee member of only one financial institution in a particular industry.

Pakistan. Pakistan has adopted an unusual three-tier *Shari'a*-compliance structure to ensure "deep and extensive" supervision of *Shari'a* compliance. The structure consists of the following components: (1) internal *Shari'a* advisers for Islamic banks, (2) a national *Shari'a*-compliance inspection unit, and (3) a national *Shari'a* advisory board established by the State Bank of Pakistan, the central bank (Akhtar 2006).

The *Shari'a* board established by Pakistan's central bank is the final authority on all matters pertaining to Islamic finance in the country. A member of the national *Shari'a* advisory board is allowed to serve concurrently as a *Shari'a* adviser of a financial institution, unlike the rules promulgated in Malaysia. But similar to the Malaysian system, a *Shari'a* adviser can serve only one financial institution at a time (Hasan, Zulkifli, 2007).

Kuwait. The Central Bank of Kuwait regulates Islamic banking institutions domiciled in the country under the Central Bank of Kuwait Law of 1968. Kuwaiti banks are required to have an independent *Shari'a* advisory board when applying for registration under Article 93 of the 1968 law. Each bank's advisory board is required to have at least three members, all of whom are appointed by the Central Bank of Kuwait. A financial institution must thoroughly disclose in its memorandum of agreement and articles of association presented to the Central Bank of Kuwait details governing the creation, jurisdiction, and procedures of its advisory board.

Conflicts of opinion among members of an institution's *Shari'a* advisory board concerning a *Shari'a* ruling may be referred by the board of directors of the institution to the Fatwa Board in the Ministry of Awqaf and Islamic Affairs, which is the final arbiter. A bank's advisory board is required to submit to its board of directors an annual report listing its opinions on the bank's operations with regard to *Shari'a* compliance. This report then becomes part of the bank's annual report. A bank's *Shari'a* advisory board reports directly to the Ministry of Awqaf and Islamic Affairs, not to the Central Bank of Kuwait. Islamic scholars may serve concurrently on the *Shari'a* advisory committees of more than one financial institution.

Bahrain. In Bahrain, financial institutions are required to establish their own *Shari'a* supervisory committees and comply with the Bahrain-based Accounting and Auditing Organization of Islamic Financial Institutions' "Governance Standards for Islamic Financial Institutions No. 1 and No. 2." The Central Bank of Bahrain has established a national *Shari'a* board, but the jurisdiction of this board is limited to verification of *Shari'a* compliance in the central bank's activities.[23]

United Arab Emirates. The Higher Shari'ah Authority supervises Islamic financial institutions in the United Arab Emirates (UAE) to ensure that transactions are compatible with the principles of *Shari'a*. It is the final authority on all matters relating to Islamic finance. The Higher Shari'ah Authority was established under Article 5 of Federal Law No. 6 (1985).[24] The 1985 law requires that each financial institution domiciled in the UAE form a *Shari'a* supervisory board with a minimum of three members whose appointments must meet the approval of the Higher Shari'ah Authority.[25]

Qatar. Islamic banks in Qatar have their own *Shari'a* advisory boards. *Shari'a* advisory board members are not restricted from serving on the board of more than one financial institution (Hasan, Aznan bin, 2007). The Qatar Central Bank does not have a national *Shari'a* advisory board; it appoints *Shari'a* scholars to issue rulings on a case-by-case basis. The Supreme Shari'a Council at the Awqaf Ministry may arbitrate disputes.

International Islamic Standard-Setting Bodies

A number of multilateral institutions issue standards and best practice guidelines not necessarily related to *Shari'a* compliance for the rapidly growing but fragmented Islamic financial industry. These standards and guidelines are not legally binding, but they may become mandatory if approved by national regulatory authorities.

---

[23] For more on Bahrain Islamic Bank, see Islamic Finance News Portal posts: http://islamicfinanceupdates.wordpress.com/tag/bahrain-islamic-bank.

[24] See http://centralbank.ae/pdf/LawNo6-1985-IslaminBanks.pdf.

[25] For more on these policies, see the Central Bank of the UAE at www.centralbank.ae.

Compliance with such standards helps an institution achieve a good reputation globally and win customer confidence. The international standard-setting bodies also help governments and supervisory agencies gain a better understanding of the marketplace and may play a key role in promoting financial stability across the markets.

The goals of the international Islamic standard-setting organizations are as follows:

- to promote good corporate governance, enhance transparency, and strengthen market discipline;
- to support research and development in areas that are critical for financial stability; and
- to provide a platform for regulators and interested stakeholders to discuss and share expertise and experiences.

Exhibit 7.3 outlines the governing purpose and mission of the major international Islamic standard-setting bodies.

Challenges to Effective Islamic Corporate Governance

Developing a strong framework for governance, supervision, and regulation of Islamic banks is a challenge for the Islamic financial industry today. In this section, we discuss several topics that are necessary for achieving best practices in Islamic corporate governance as highlighted by Nafis and Shanmugam (2007) and Akhtar (2006).

An Internationally Recognized Regulatory System. Significant fragmentation exists among the countries with Islamic financial institutions as to the scope of corporate governance and regulation of these institutions. The ability of Islamic banks and financial institutions to grow and compete globally requires the establishment of an internationally accepted regulatory body. Some countries have adopted the view that Islamic banks should be subject to a supervisory and regulatory regime that is separate from that of conventional banks. Other countries, however, see no problem with having Islamic banks and conventional banks regulated under the same regime, although they recognize the distinctiveness of Islamic banking. The UAE, Qatar, and Malaysia are among the countries that have adopted a single regulatory system.

A Level Playing Field. In many non-Muslim countries, Islamic and conventional institutions are not on a level playing field because of the different nature of financial contracts that Islamic institutions use and the required legal documentation, regulatory requirements, and *Shari'a*-enforcement rules. At present, most Islamic banks, whether in Muslim or non-Muslim countries, operate under a dual banking system; the exceptions are Iran and Sudan, which allow only Islamic banks. Until a single international regulatory framework for Islamic banking is adopted, continued growth of Islamic banking and financing—especially in countries with dual banking systems—requires the creation and maintenance of a level playing field for Islamic and conventional financial institutions.

Exhibit 7.3. Primary International Islamic Standard-Setting Organizations

AAOIFI	The Accounting and Auditing Organization for Islamic Financial Institutions prepares and issues accounting, auditing, and corporate governance standards, as well as ethics and *Shari'a* standards, for Islamic financial institutions. It has also planned a Certified Islamic Public Accountant program for accountancy education. www.aaoifi.com
IFSB	The Islamic Financial Services Board serves as an international standard-setting body for regulatory and supervisory agencies. It has pronounced on corporate governance, risk management, capital adequacy, supervisory review processes, transparency, market discipline, recognition of ratings on *Shari'a*-compliant financial instruments, and the development of money markets. It also arranges summits, conferences, and workshops on issues relating to Islamic banking. www.ifsb.org
MASB	The Malaysian Accounting Standards Board's primary role is to develop accounting and financial reporting standards. Its financial reporting standards are developed in harmony with the international accounting standards organization and the AAOIFI. The standards are developed specifically to meet the needs of Islamic financial practices as well as the needs of the regulatory and economic structure in Malaysia. www.masb.org.my
GCIBFI	The General Council for Islamic Banks and Financial Institutions is an international autonomous not-for-profit corporate body that represents Islamic banks and financial institutions globally. Its key aims are as follows: • disseminating information on *Shari'a* concepts and the rules and provisions related to them in order to help develop the Islamic financial industry, • enhancing cooperation among its members, • providing information related to Islamic financial institutions, and • promoting the interests of its members and helping them overcome common difficulties and challenges.
IIFM	The International Islamic Financial Market is one of the core infrastructure institutions of the Islamic financial industry. The not-for-profit organization was founded jointly by the central banks and monetary authorities of Bahrain, Brunei, Indonesia, Malaysia, and Sudan and the Islamic Development Bank (Jeddah, Saudi Arabia). Its primary function is to enhance cooperation among Islamic countries and their financial institutions, specifically in promoting trading in the secondary market for *Shari'a*-compliant financial instruments. www.iifm.net
IIRA	The Islamic International Rating Agency started operations in July 2005 with the aim of assisting the development of regional financial markets. It assesses the risk profiles of market participants and financial instruments to help inform investor decision making. www.iirating.com
LMC	The Liquidity Management Centre seeks to develop an active secondary market for short-term *Shari'a*-compliant treasury products. It helps Islamic financial institutions effectively manage their asset/liability mismatch and improve the quality of their portfolios.
BIS	The Bank for International Settlements of Basel, Switzerland, fosters international monetary and financial cooperation and serves as a bank for central banks. This international body has issued guidelines to mitigate supervisory issues and improve the quality of banking supervision worldwide. Like conventional banks, Islamic financial banks have to comply with Basel and Basel II guidelines. www.bis.org
IMF	The International Monetary Fund was established to promote international monetary cooperation, financial stability, and arrangements for reforming the international financial system. Among its goals are to foster economic growth and support high levels of employment. It also provides temporary financial assistance to countries to help ease balance of payment problems. www.imf.org

Risk Management. *Shari'a* compliance procedures and risk management in Islamic financial institutions are currently hampered by discrepancies in interpretation by the *Shari'a* supervisory boards of the individual financial institutions and by the lack of a single Islamic financial regulatory body.

As we have noted, the Islamic financial model is built around the concept of risk sharing between the provider and user of funds. Thus, investment risk must be managed. Although profit-and-loss sharing may shift risks to investment account holders and bank depositors, it may also expose the Islamic banks themselves to risks normally borne by equity investors. Also, with the blurring of the distinction between depositor and equityholder in the profit-and-loss–sharing model, the bank may have an increased exposure to risk because this model has no concept of a borrower being in default (with an exception of negligence or mismanagement), so the bank may or may not have ways to recover collateral, as is possible in conventional banking.

Disclosure and Transparency. Information disclosure is crucial in an Islamic financial environment because of the absence of protection for investment account holders and bank depositors. Aside from helping Islamic bank stakeholders make reasonably informed business and investment decisions and enabling depositors and creditors to monitor a bank's performance, adequate disclosure also helps oversight bodies exercise effective supervision of banks and other financial institutions.

Additional disclosure is needed in the areas of bank administrative policies, investment strategies, and financial performance. Customers should be informed on a consistent and timely basis about the bank's methods of profit calculation, its asset allocation decisions, and the mechanics of return smoothing (if any) in their investment accounts.

Islamic financial institutions should also be transparent in their adoption and application of *Shari'a* principles and rules issued by religious scholars and in disclosing information about the structure of products and the products' strengths and weaknesses. This issue has been debated with increasing vigor within the Muslim community.

Responsibility and Accountability of *Shari'a* Supervisory Body. The demarcation needed in a conventional bank between the board of directors and the managers has an analogy in Islamic finance—namely, the demarcation needed between the role and functions of the *Shari'a* advisory committee or special *Shari'a* board and the management of the Islamic bank. Because of the faith-based nature of the business, the *Shari'a* adviser will obviously review most aspects of the businesses, but the involvement should focus on approval of the basic structure of products and other special activities, not the day-to-day operations of the business. The *Shari'a* adviser, however, has to be more involved than an outside board member or adviser in a conventional bank.

©2009 The Research Foundation of CFA Institute

Shortage of *Shari'a* Scholars. Not enough *Shari'a* scholars with financial expertise exist to engage in the kind of careful oversight that Islamic banking requires. Thus, the pool of overseers trained in both *Shari'a* and finance must be increased (Khir, Gupta, and Shanmugam 2007).

The shortage of sufficiently qualified *Shari'a* scholars means that in countries where it is allowed, scholars often serve concurrently on the *Shari'a* supervisory boards of a number of firms. This practice raises concerns about a board's ability to exercise effective oversight of a firm's products and services by rigorously challenging them when necessary. Also at issue is the inevitable conflict of interest when a firm's *Shari'a* advisory board is responsible for both the annual *Shari'a* audit and the approval of products for *Shari'a* compliance. Some regulatory bodies have worked to address these concerns in a move toward better governance policies, but many have not.

Summary

Adopting strong corporate governance practices is vital to the success of conventional and Islamic banks and financial institutions. If the Islamic financial industry is to continue to grow and garner additional market share in the competitive global financial industry, widespread adoption of corporate governance best practice is imperative. The Islamic finance model, built on the Islamic religious principle of risk and profit sharing on an *ex post* basis, will benefit from increased transparency and improved disclosure of operations. The moral teachings of Islam, such as accountability, trustworthiness, and transparency, apply to its followers in all aspects of their lives, including their professional pursuits, and in the context of institutional responsibility, not individual responsibility alone. Nevertheless, an Islamic bank or financial institution must also adopt internationally acceptable corporate governance practices, operate with the oversight of the relevant national and supranational regulatory bodies, and obey applicable regulations and laws.

Chapter 8. Future Outlook and Challenges for Islamic Finance

Islamic financial institutions are growing rapidly. For example, Noor Islamic Bank was launched by the government of Dubai with US$1 billion in capital in early 2008. The bank began operations with 10 branches but expects to increase its market share of Islamic banking in the United Arab Emirates (UAE) to as much as 50 percent (Walid 2008). In April 2008, when Saudi Arabia launched the government-backed Inma Bank, it raised US$2.8 billion in capital in an initial public offering. The establishment of these large Islamic banks, partly with state backing, is a departure for Islamic finance, which until recently was dominated by hundreds of small institutions.

With no significant assets four decades ago, the Islamic banking industry now accounts for 15–20 percent of the banking market across the Organization of the Islamic Conference (OIC) countries (Ahmad 2008). Islamic banking assets are expected to exceed US$1 trillion by 2010 ("Morgan Stanley Says . . ." 2008). Some reports suggest that assets could rise by 17 percent a year to US$1.3 trillion by 2012 (Zinkin 2008). The current tally of Islamic financial institutions stands at more than 300 in 75 countries (Mittal 2008).

Some reports state that Islamic banking assets in the Asia Pacific area account for as much as US$450 billion, which amounts to 60 percent of the global Islamic banking market. The numbers are expected to grow (Nyee 2009). Indeed, prospects for Islamic finance in general are good. The International Monetary Fund expects Islamic finance to keep expanding, despite the global financial turbulence, because of the pool of liquidity in the oil-rich states of the Persian Gulf and the unabated appetite of Muslim investors for Islamic financial products (Kilner 2008).

Four locations—Kuala Lumpur in Malaysia, Dubai, Bahrain, and London—have their sights set on being the global center for Islamic finance. Kuala Lumpur is widely regarded as the hub of Islamic finance in Asia, whereas London is likely to emerge as the gateway for the industry in Europe. Malaysia has long been an established Islamic financial center, but it has been challenged in recent years by strong growth in the Persian Gulf driven primarily by huge oil-related revenues.

Challenges Arising from Interpretation of *Shari'a*

Shari'a is open to interpretation, and religious scholars on *Shari'a* advisory boards frequently hold different views on key issues. The existence of diverse interpretations of Islamic principles has resulted in a lack of standardization in Islamic finance. In many countries, each financial institution relies on its own *Shari'a* board to review products. Different scholars can disagree on what is "Islamic."

The varying interpretations of *Shari'a* can be attributed primarily to the five different schools of Islamic thought—Shafi'i, Shia, Hanafi, Hanbali, and Maliki. A *Shari'a* board thus has considerable discretion in the interpretation of Islamic law and may choose any school of thought to inform its decision-making process.

In Malaysia, scholars place priority on form over substance when deciding whether a particular product is *Shari'a* compliant. Scholars in the Gulf Cooperation Council (GCC) countries, however, contend that *Shari'a* compliance is determined by the intent of the transaction.[26] Conservative investors in the Middle East are uncomfortable with the principles of *Shari'a* followed in Malaysia. Such investors view Malaysia's interpretation of *Shari'a* as more flexible than is typical in the Arab world.

The lack of standardized religious decisions leads to uncertainty, confusion, and unease among scholars and investors. This situation restricts the industry from reaching its potential because a number of inefficiencies arise from the lack of standardization. For example, different interpretations of *Shari'a* mean that one Islamic bank may not be able to accept or use as a model another Islamic bank's products, which can stifle the integration of Islamic finance at both the national and international levels.

Controversy over acceptable transactions can also hinder the development of certain products or market segments. For example, in late 2007, Sheikh Muhammad Taqi Usmani, a prominent religious scholar who heads the Bahrain-based Accounting and Auditing Organization for Islamic Financial Institutions (AAOIFI), jolted the industry by criticizing *sukuk* (Islamic bonds) as being "un-Islamic" (Halim 2007). He argued that they were akin to conventional interest-bearing bonds because risk was not shared among the parties involved. Until that criticism, most *Shari'a* scholars had approved the controversial structure as they sought to expand the market.

In mid-2008, Usmani clarified that he was criticizing two specific bond structures—*musyarakah* (partnership financing) and *mudharabah* (trust financing)—for breaking key principles of Islamic law. He was not criticizing the *ijarah* (leasing) structure that involves a sale and leaseback arrangement (for a refresher on *sukuk* structures, see Chapter 4). Furthermore, he specified that his guidance was for future reference and did not affect the existing US$80 billion in outstanding *sukuk*. Nevertheless, the market reacted when Usmani made his pronouncement. This reaction and future similar reactions to the opinions of religious scholars reduce confidence in the market, add to market volatility, and reduce the value of securities.

---

[26]The GCC consists of Bahrain, Kuwait, Oman, Qatar, Saudi Arabia, and the United Arab Emirates.

Need for Harmonization of Islamic Banking Standards

Greater consensus on standards and product design in the Islamic financial system is required before the system can fully mature. Not only will greater standardization increase scalability of services and industry efficiencies, but without greater standardization in certain core products and markets, Islamic banks will struggle to develop the volumes enjoyed by their conventional banking counterparts. Suggestions include the formation of *Shari'a* advisory boards at the national and international levels and for the creation of a council—representing the five Islamic schools of thought—that would decide as a single body what types of financial services conform to Islamic law and would define cohesive rules to expedite the process of introducing new products (Ahmed 2007).

The AAOIFI is working hard to develop common regulatory standards for Islamic financial institutions and to carry out *Shari'a* training. The AAOIFI states that more than 16 jurisdictions follow or consult its standards, which take into consideration all the Islamic schools of thought. The AAOIFI standards are not enforceable, however, so different scholars within the same jurisdiction may continue to produce divergent opinions.

Similarly, the Malaysia-based Islamic Financial Services Board (IFSB), established in 2002, has issued standards and guidelines pertaining to capital adequacy, risk management, and corporate governance for institutions offering Islamic financial services (other than *takaful*, or Islamic insurance). The IFSB maintains that the adoption of such standards will lead to harmonization of *Shari'a* interpretations, promote homogeneity in the Islamic finance industry, and enhance investor protections. Like the AAOIFI, the IFSB has no enforcement powers.

Without the consensus of a single regulatory, accounting, and *Shari'a*-compliance framework, the expansion of Islamic finance into Muslim countries with large populations and great potential, such as Indonesia, can proceed only at an unnecessarily slow pace.

Other Challenges Facing Islamic Banking

In addition to the issues associated with varying interpretations of *Shari'a* and a lack of regulatory standardization, Islamic finance faces other challenges.

The first challenge is dealing with the charge that Islamic financial products are "*Shari'a* synthetics"; that is, the products are basically copies of conventional products that are structured in a way that makes them appear to be *Shari'a* compliant. These critics assert that new products increasingly contravene the *spirit* of Islamic finance. Products such as derivatives and hedge funds, for example, are considered particularly controversial, given the Quran's ban on *gharar* (speculation). Critics argue that Islamic banking needs to "innovate within" and develop more of its own products to avoid imitating conventional financial instruments.

In contrast, given that the industry is relatively young and that many of its products are still nascent, others question how much product innovation is actually needed at the moment. They stress that the market is as much in need of consolidation and refinement as it is of innovation and new products.

Second, Islamic financial institutions are challenged to offer better customer service—service that matches international standards—and also to invest in effective technology, such as using the internet to create new distribution channels to reach more customers. Such concepts as "quality" and "creating value for customers" are central to the success of banks entering the Islamic market today. A step toward meeting this challenge is the move by Noor Islamic Bank in the UAE to offer a bank service delivered through post offices, which targets the 50 percent of the population in that country with no formal bank account. The new service is expected to attract low-paid workers, including many expatriates from such countries as India, Pakistan, and the Philippines, who represent a significant part of the UAE's workforce.

Third, proponents of Islamic finance are concerned about the current environment and future regulatory regimes in terms of the treatment of conventional banks versus the treatment of Islamic banks. Separate supervision and regulation of Islamic banks have yet to take hold in most countries; only Kuwait and Bahrain operate separate regulatory regimes for the sector at this time. In most markets, Islamic banks follow the standards set by local regulators for conventional banks, even if those standards are not always appropriate for Islamic institutions.

Fourth, the shortage of skilled and well-trained professionals is limiting the ability of Islamic banks to compete and expand market share. The industry needs new talent and needs to retrain conventional bankers in the practices of Islamic banking. A few educational institutions offer specialized degrees in Islamic finance, but the demand is overwhelming the supply of graduates. The arguments are being made that universities should offer master's programs (MBA and PhD programs) that focus on Islamic finance and that a globally recognized professional certification should be created.

Fifth, the industry needs universally accepted terminology to aid communication across the broad expanse of the Muslim community.

Sixth, Islamic financial institutions need to increase investment in research and development, including products and mechanisms related to risk management. Development of the investment side of the Islamic finance market has been rapid, but *Shari'a*-compliant risk management for Islamic finance has evolved at a slower pace. As Islamic financial institutions expand beyond national borders, they need sophisticated tools to manage the risks associated with diversified portfolios and global customer servicing. Islamic derivatives may provide answers to many of the industry's risk management needs; thus, they are being aggressively pursued. Meanwhile, however, some analysts would like to see banks build links to top-quality academic institutions to support research on Islamic banking and finance.

Finally, replacing Arabic terminology with comparable terms used in conventional banking has been discussed as a way to appeal to non-Muslim customers. A change of this type would also facilitate comparisons between Islamic and conventional financial products. Islamic finance appeals to non-Muslim investors who are not keen to invest in securities that could be potentially harmful to human beings, such as the equity or debt of tobacco, alcohol, and gambling companies. Thus, a market exists if the industry can reach it.

The Future of Islamic Finance

Figure 8.1 shows two paths of the Islamic finance industry—one at 10 percent growth leading to US$1.2 trillion by 2010 (and US$1.8 trillion by 2015) and one at 15 percent growth leading to US$1.4 trillion by 2010 (US$2.8 trillion by 2015). Drivers of global growth in Islamic finance are expected to be growth in Western countries, acceptance of *takaful*, and improvements in the sector as financial institutions deal with the challenges noted in this chapter.

In several Western jurisdictions, nonbanking Islamic financial services (specifically, mortgages) are expected to continue to grow steadily, particularly if regulators pursue the principle of "social inclusion" as part of the goals of the financial sector. In the United Kingdom, HSBC was the first major bank to offer mortgages (in

Figure 8.1. Projected Size of the Islamic Finance Industry

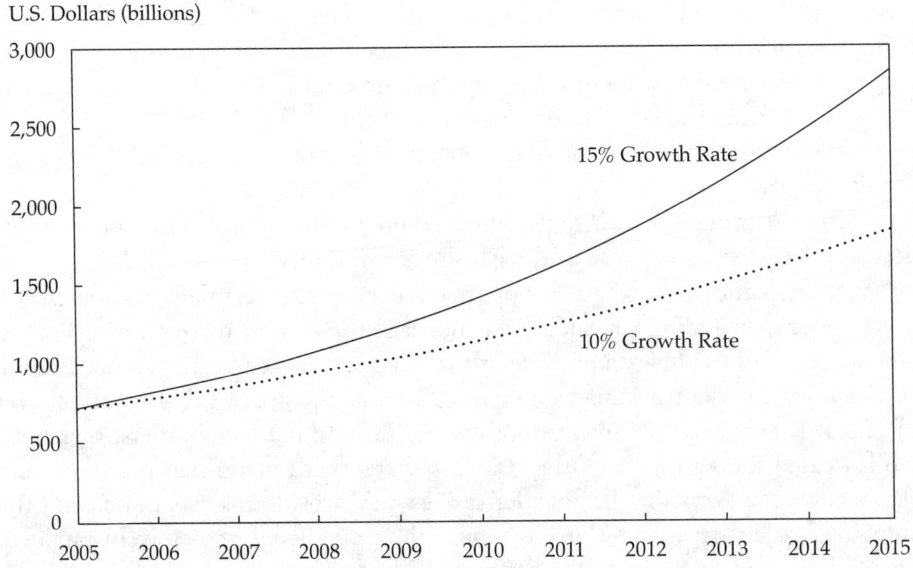

Source: Islamic Financial Services Board (2007).

2003) that comply with Islamic law. The country's first purely Islamic bank, the Islamic Bank of Britain, opened for business the following year, 2004. Her Majesty's Treasury and the Bank of England have been encouraging Islamic mortgages, investments, and current accounts in the United Kingdom. The market research group Datamonitor has predicted that the Islamic mortgage market in the United Kingdom could climb to about US$2.2 billion in 2009 from US$260 million in 2005. The United Kingdom has nearly 2 million Muslims ("Sharia Mortgage Market Continues to Grow" 2008).

Future growth in Islamic finance will also be helped by the robust outlook for *takaful*, which is receiving growing acceptance by Muslims despite some criticism it has received. Islamic insurance is an underdeveloped market in certain regions, particularly the Persian Gulf area. Familiarity with *takaful* is helping to reduce Muslim suspicion about paying premiums, however, which has traditionally stunted growth in the conservative Persian Gulf countries.

Population growth and new government regulations, including mandatory corporate insurance schemes, are expected to make the *takaful* sector one of the fastest growing sectors in the next few years; it will quadruple by 2013. In the past five years, several *takaful* companies have entered the market, and they now represent almost 10 percent of the 280 insurance companies in the region. In the UAE, the government is pursuing mandatory health insurance that should drive the industry's development (Ernst & Young 2007).

Finally, industry players acknowledge the challenges discussed previously and are working to deal with them. Islamic banking, in particular, emerged on the scene only a little more than four decades ago and faces the challenges of a young industry. But the AAOIFI and IFSB are on a mission to promote better transparency in Islamic banking and to provide regulatory guidance across the global Islamic finance landscape.

Summary

Despite the challenges facing the Islamic finance industry, the future looks promising indeed. The combination of a large untapped Muslim population, a significant increase in the oil-related wealth of high-net-worth individuals from the Middle East, and religiously inspired demand has created a significant target market for Islamic financial institutions. As the range of *Shari'a*-compliant products and services expands, the ability of firms to offer competitive returns to clients also expands.

The obstacles currently preventing faster spread of Islamic financial products and acting as a drag on industry growth are being addressed by the major market players. These institutions are aware of the need for greater standardization within product lines and for better and more consistent regulation and governance if the industry is to flourish and be competitive with the conventional banking and financial industry.

Glossary

akhlaq = ethical code

al-ijarah thumma al-bai (AITAB*)* = an *ijarah* (leasing) contract combined with a *bai* (purchase) contract

al-ujrah = fee for safekeeping assets

amal salih = virtuous act

amanah = trust

aqad = agreements

aqidah = creed

aquila = mutual agreement or joint guarantee to spread the financial liability or risk of a member

ayah = verses in *sura* (singular = *ayat*)

bai contract = sales/purchase contract

bai' al-naqdi = buying and selling on a cash basis

bai' bithaman ajil contract = deferred-payment sale

bai' inah contract = sale-and-buyback contract

bai' istijrar contract = supplier contract

bai' istisna contract = order sale contract

bai' mu'ajjal contract = deferred-payment sale

bai' salam contract = deferred-payment sale or forward sale contract (used primarily in agriculture)

batil contract = void contract

bezant = gold currency

diyah = blood money

eid al-fitr = prayer ending Ramadan

faraid = inheritance law

fasid contract = invalid contract

fatwa = religious opinions

fiqh-al-muamalat = commercial law

gharar = uncertainty, risk, or speculation

ghayr lazim contract = a contract that either party may terminate

hadith = oral traditions relating to the words and deeds of Muhammad

hajji = pilgrimage

halal = permissible

haram = prohibited

harus = permissible act

heyal = ruses

hibah = gift awarded by a bank without any commensurate exchange

hiwalah = remittance involving a transfer of funds/debt from the depositor's/debtor's account to the receiver's/creditor's account

ibadah = worship

ibadat = human-to-God relationship

ibra = rebate

ijab = offer

ijarah financing = leasing

ijarah muntahia bittamleek = buyback leasing

ijarah thumma bai = leasing and subsequent purchase

ijarah wa iqtina = lease contract with a put and/or call option on the leased asset held by the customer

ijma = to determine or agree to

istihsan = personal interpretation

istislah = method to solve a problem

itjihad = striving (to adapt to law)

jaiz contract = a contract that either party may terminate

jualah contract = unilateral contract for a task (e.g., wage or stipend)

kafalah contract = guaranteed contract

khianat = betrayal

khilafah = trusteeship

lazim contract = binding and irrevocable contract

maal = wealth

maisir = gambling

makruh = discouraged act

mandub = commendable act

maslahah = the beliefs of Muslims

maslahat = in the public interest

mawkuf contract = valid but suspended contract

muamalat = human-to-human relationships

mubah = permissible act

mudarib = agent (usually, bank) for the investor

mudharabah = profit sharing or trust financing

mudharabah muqayyadah = special investment account

mudharabah mutlaqah = general investment account

muqasah = set-offs

murabahah = trading

murabahah contract = cost-plus-profit or cost-plus-markup contract

musaqat = arrangement between, for example, a farmer and a worker who agrees to water the garden or both share in the harvest

musharka = a type of profit sharing

musyarakah = joint venture or partnership financing or equity participation

musyarakah mutanaqisah = diminishing partnership

nafidh contract = immediate contract

neaa = sincerity

qabul = acceptance in a contract

qard = interest-free loan payable on demand

qard hassan = literally, "good or benevolent loan," a gratuitous or charitable contract, or free loan with no profit (markup)

qiyas = precedents

Quran = Muslim holy book

rabb–ul-mal = silent-partner investor

rahnu = collateralized financing

riba = the giving or receiving of interest

sahih contract = valid contract

salaam = submission or peace

salam = deferred sale

Shari'a = Islamic principles or law

sukuk = Islamic bonds (singular is *sakk*)

sukuk al-musyarakah = investment *sukuk*

Sunnah = sayings of the Prophet Muhammad

sunnat = commendable act

sura = chapters in Quran (singular is *surat*)

taawun = brotherhood or mutual assistance

tabarru' = donation, gift, or contribution

takaful = Islamic insurance

taqwa = righteousness

tawarruq = structure for cash financing

tawhid = the need to submit fully to God

ujr = fee

ummah = overarching global Muslim community or society

urbun contract = sale in which the buyer deposits money in advance

'urf = custom

wa'd = binding promise in Islamic law

wadiah contract = safekeeping contract (e.g., savings account)

wajib = obligatory act

wakalah = delegation or representation; when an agent receives a management fee; when another person acts, usually for a fee

wakalah with *waqf* = a form of the *wakalah* that uses a foundation (*waqf*)

wasiyat = will

zakat = religious tithe

zakat fitr = *zakat* (religious tithe) due from the start of Ramadan until the prayer ending Ramadan (*eid al-fitr*)

References

Abdullah, Mohd Asri bin. 2005. "Being a Good Muslim and Its Relation to Corporate Social Responsibility." Paper presented at 16th JPA-BMCC Management Development Programme, Kuala Lumpur, Malaysia (1 July).

Adawiah, Engku Rabiah. 2007. "Applied Shari'ah in Financial Transactions." Paper presented at the Global Islamic Finance Forum, Kuala Lumpur Convention Centre (26–29 March): http://ribh.files.wordpress.com/2007/10/applied-shariah-in-financial-transactions.pdf.

Ahmad, Ausaf. 1993. "Contemporary Practices of Islamic Financing Techniques." Research Paper No. 20, Islamic Research and Training Institute, Islamic Development Bank, Jeddah, Saudi Arabia.

Ahmad, Ferdous. 2008. "Islamic Banking Blooms in Bangladesh." Islam Online (26 June): www.islamonline.net/servlet/Satellite?c=Article_C&cid=1213871353774&pagename=Zone-English-News/NWELayout.

Ahmed, Elwaleed M. 2007. "A Unified Voice: The Role of Shariah Advisory Boards in Islamic Finance." *Business Islamica* (October): available at http://theroleofshariahadvisoryboards.blogspot.com.

Akhtar, Shamshad. 2006. "Syariah Compliant Corporate Governance." Keynote address by the governor of the State Bank of Pakistan at the annual Corporate Governance Conference, Dubai, United Arab Emirates.

Alhabshi, Syed Musa. 2007. "Optimal Shariah Governance in Islamic Finance: Reporting Perspective." Paper presented to the Global Islamic Finance Forum, Kuala Lumpur, Malaysia (28 March).

Al-Huda. 2008. Bimonthly online magazine of Al Huda Center of Islamic Banking and Economics, no. 031 (1 September–1 October): www.alhudacibe.com/AlhudaMagazine/Issue-031/index.php.

Ali, M., and A.A. Sarkar. 1995. "Islamic Banking: Principles and Operational Methodology." *Thoughts on Economics*, vol. 5, no. 3–4 (July–December):20–25 (Dhaka, Bangladesh: Islamic Economics Research Bureau.).

Al-Jarhi, M.A. No date. *Islamic Finance: An Efficient & Equitable Option*. Jeddah, Saudi Arabia: The Islamic Research and Training Institute.

Al Maraj, Rasheed M. 2008. Welcome by the governor of the Central Bank of Bahrain at World Islamic Funds & Capital Markets Conference 2008, Manama, Bahrain (26 May): www.cbb.gov.bh/cmsrule/index.jsp?action=article&ID=2944.

Al-Omar, Fuad, and Mohammed Abdel-Haq. 1996. *Islamic Banking: Theory, Practices and Challenges*. New York: Palgrave Macmillan.

Al-Qari, Abdul Aziz. No date. "Aqeedah, Its Meaning and Importance." Published by Dar Makkah, Islaam.com (www.islaam.com/Article.aspx?id=65).

AmBank Group. 2008. "Developments in the Global Islamic Funds Industry." In *Islamic Finance News Asset & Wealth Management Guide 2008* (www.islamicfinancenews.com/supplement_2008_a&w.asp).

AMMB. 2006. "AMMB Holdings Berhad Annual Report 2006" (www.ambankgroup.com/ambank_corporate.asp?sc=ambg_investor_ relations& pg=ambg_investor_annual_reports&sub=ambg_report_archive_2006&subp-am bg_report_archive).

Archer, S., R.A. Abdel Karim, and T. Al-Deehani. 1998. "Financial Contracting, Governance Structures and the Accounting Regulation of Islamic Banks: An Analysis in Terms of Agency Theory and Transaction Cost Economics." *Journal of Management and Governance*, vol. 2, no. 2:149–170.

Asian Banker Research. 2008. "Riding the Winds of Change in Islamic Banking." Paper presented at the Asian Banker Forum, Kuala Lumpur, Malaysia (20 August).

Augustine, B.D. 2008. "Standing Up and Being Counted." *Gulf News* (26 May): www.gulfnews.com/gnqfr/gnqfr22008/bankingfinance/10216032.html.

Ayub, Muhammad. 2007. Understanding Islamic Finance. Chichester, U.K.: John Wiley and Sons.

Bakar, Mohd Daud. 2005. "Islamic Derivative Solutions: Methodology, Issues and Product Structuring with Special Reference to Profit Rate Swap and Forward Forex." Presentation to the Seminar on Islamic Finance (http://iimm.bnm.gov.my/idb/schedule.htm).

Bank Islam Malaysia. 1994. *Islamic Banking Practice: From the Practitioner's Perspective*. Kuala Lumpur, Malaysia: Pelanduk Publications.

Bank Negara Malaysia. 2004. "The 2003 Bank Negara Malaysia Annual Report" (26 March): www.bnm.gov.my/view.php?dbIndex=0&website_id=1&id=455.

———. 2005. "Malaysian Takaful Industry 1984–2004" (www.bnm.gov.my/files/publication/tkf/en/2004/booklet.en.pdf).

———. 2008. "Bank Negara Malaysia Annual Report 2007" (26 March): www.bnm.gov.my/index.php?ch=109&pg=333&ac=44.

Bhatty, Ajmal. 2008. "Will Takaful Penetration Meet Conventional Insurance?" Paper presented at the Second Annual Takaful Summit, Knightsbridge, London (www.whatstakaful.com/people/ajmalbhatty.pdf).

Billah, Mohd. Ma'sum. 2006. *Shar'iah Standard of Business Contract*. Kuala Lumpur, Malaysia: A.S. Noordeen.

Björklund, Iréne, and Lisbeth Lundstrom. 2004. "Islamic Banking: An Alternative System." Kristianstad University (December).

Bowman, Dylan. 2008. "Takaful Industry to Top $15bn in Ten Years." *Arabian Business.com* (15 April): www.arabianbusiness.com/516591-takaful-industry-to-top-isbn-in-ten-years.

Collins, Charles M. 1881. *The History, Law, and Practice of Banking*. London: James Cornish & Sons.

Cook, Vince. 2008. "Across the Miles from the GCC into Asia." *Gulf News* (26 May): www.gulfnews.com/gnqfr/gnqfr22008/bankingfinance/10216034.html.

Dauphine, Paris. 2007. "Islamic Finance: Market Developments & Opportunities." Presentation to the conference Global Financial Services (16 May).

De Ramos, Rita Raagas. 2009. "Sharia Assets Total a Mere $65 Billion Worldwide." *Asian Investor* (9 January): www.asianinvestor.net/article.aspx?CIID=132521.

"Dubai Forms Islamic Banking Body." 2008. ArabianBusiness.com (12 June): www.arabianbusiness.com/520386-dubai-forms-islamic-banking-body.

Eaves, Elisabeth. 2008. "God and Mammon." *Forbes* (28 April): www.forbes.com/2008/04/21/islamic-banking-interest-islamic-finance-cx_ee_islamicfinance08_0421intro.html.

Ebrahim, M. Shahid, and Tan Kai Joo. 2001. "Islamic Banking in Brunei Darussalam." *International Journal of Social Economics*, vol. 28, no. 4:314–337.

El-Gamal, Mahmoud. 2006. *Islamic Finance: Law, Economics, and Practice*. New York: Cambridge University Press.

Enayat, H. 2005. *Modern Islamic Political Thought*. I.B. Tauris: London.

Ernst & Young. 2007. "The World Takaful Report."

Ghani, Badlisyah Abdul. 2004. "Islamic Profit Rate Swap—Its Mechanics and Objectives." Seminar on Derivatives in Islamic Finance, Islamic Interbank Money Market (24 June): http://iimm.bnm.gov.my/index.php?ch=20&pg=66.

Goitein, S.D. 1971. *A Mediterranean Society*. Berkley: University of California Press.

Grail Research. 2007. "Overview of Islamic Finance" (June): www.grailresearch.com/PDF/ContenPodsPdf/Islamic_Finance_Overview.pdf.

Grierson, Philip. 1999. *Byzantine Coinage*. Washington, DC: Dumbarton Oaks Research Library and Collection.

Gulaid, M.A. 1995. "Financing Agriculture through Islamic Modes and Instruments: Practical Scenario and Applicability." Research Paper No. 34, Islamic Research Training Institute, Islamic Development Bank.

Halim, Nazneen. 2007. "Islamic Finance Report Are GCC Sukuk Tainted?" *Islamic Finance News*, vol. 4, no. 48 (30 November).

Haneef, Rafe. 2005. "RM2.05 Billion Islamic Residential Mortgage Backed Securities (Sukuk al-Musyarakah)." Paper presented at the Islamic Banking Conference, Karachi, India (September).

Haron, S., and B. Shanmugam. 1997. *Islamic Banking System: Concepts and Applications*. Petaling Jaya, Malaysia: Pelanduk Publications.

Hasan, Aznan bin. 2007. "Optimal Shariah Governance in Islamic Finance." *Islamic Finance News*, vol. 4, no. 14 (7 April).

Hasan, Zulkifli. 2007. *Syariah Governance in the Financial Institutions in Malaysia*. Kuala Lumpur, Malaysia: Islamic Science University of Malaysia.

"Home Takaful." 2007. Insurance Info (www.insuranceinfo.com.my/choose_your_takaful/things_to_note/home_takaful_policies.php?intPrefLangID=1&#content3).

Hussain, Abid. No date. "The Islamic Law Of Wills." Islaam.com (www.islaam.com/Article.aspx?id=527).

Ibrahim, Muhammad bin. 2007. "Building an Effective Legal and Regulatory Framework for Islamic Banking (IB)." Paper presented at the Financial Regulators Forum, Kuala Lumpur, Malaysia (29 March): www.bnm.gov.my/microsites/giff2007/pdf/frf/06_01.pdf.

"Introduction of Islamic Variable Rate Mechanism." No date. Islamic Interbank Money Market (http://iimm.bnm.gov.my/view.php?id=6&dbIndex=0&website_id=14&ex=1212037493&md=I%85%EDW%85%0D%F3%BFb%14Oq%EC%177H).

Iqbal, M., and P. Molyneux. 2005. *Thirty Years of Islamic Banking: History, Performance and Prospects*. New York: Palgrave Macmillan.

Iqbal, Z., and H. Tsubota. 2006. "Emerging Islamic Capital Markets." *Islamic Finance*:5–11 (http://treasury.worldbank.org/web/pdf/2006EuromoneyHandbook DCM_WorldBank.pdf).

"Islamic Banking Captures 4.5% Market Share." 2008. *Daily Times* (9 December): www.dailytimes.com.pk/default.asp?page=2008\12\09\story_9-12-2008_pg5_12.

"Islamic Banking Statistics." 2008. Islamic Bankers: Resource Center (11 December): http://islamicbankers.wordpress.com/islamic-banking-statistics.

"Islamic Banks Are on the Rise." 2008. *Asian Banker Journal*, no. 76 (29 February): www.theasianbanker.com/A556C5%5CJournals.nsf/0/BB7563BAAF6 C8627482573FE0023E1DE?OpenDocument.

"Islamic Capital Market Review." 2005. *Securities Commission Annual Report 2004*. Malaysia Securities Commission (www.sc.com.my/eng/html/resources/annual/ar2004_eng/pdf/pt2_icm.pdf).

"Islamic Finance in Turkey 2009." 2009. Rationale for ICG Conference (May): www.icg-events.com/turkey/rationale.html.

Islamic Financial Services Board. 2007. "Islamic Financial Services Industry Development (Ten-Year Framework and Strategies)." Policy Dialogue Paper No. 1 (May).

"Islamic, Sharia Firms Make Up 57% of KSE Market Cap." 2009. *Kuwait Times* (1 February): www.kuwaittimes.net/read_news.php?newsid=NzUxNTAzODYw.

"Islamic Unit Trusts." 2007. *Islamic Finance News*. Bahrain Report (www.islamicfinancenews.com/supplement_2007_b.asp).

Ismail, Sufyan. 2005. "Why Islam Has Prohibited Interest and Islamic Alternatives for Financing." 1st Ethical (www.1stethical.com/downloads/TheproblemswithInterest.pdf).

Jaafar, Nik Ruslin Nik. 2007. "Islamic REITs and Capital Market Development." Paper presented at the Islamic Financial Markets Conference & Specialized Workshops, Karachi, Pakistan (24–25 January).

Kamali, Mohammad Hashim. 2005. *Principles of Islamic Jurisprudence*. 3rd ed. Cambridge, U.K.: Islamic Texts Society.

Kassim, Zainal Abidin Mohd. 2005. "*Takaful*: The Islamic Way of Insurance." *Contingencies* (January/February):33–38 (www.contingencies.org/janfeb05/0105takaful.pdf).

KFH Research. 2008. "Tapping Global High Net Worth Individuals." *Islamic Finance News*, vol. 5, no. 21 (30 May).

Khan, Afaq. 2006. "Development of Islamic Capital Markets." Presentation at Indonesia Investment Conference: Accessing the Capital Markets held in Bali, Indonesia (20–21 March): Euromoney Conferences.

Khir, Kamal, Lokesh Gupta, and Bala Shanmugam. 2007. *Islamic Banking: A Practical Perspective*. Kuala Lumpur, Malaysia: Pearson-Longman.

Kilner, Richard. 2008. "2008 to See Islamic Banking to Rise by 20%." *Banking Times* (3 January): www.bankingtimes.co.uk/03012008-2008-to-see-islamic-banking-to%20rise-by-20.

Kuo, Christine. 2008. "Islamic Finance Making Strides in Southeast Asia." *Islamic Finance News*, vol. 5, no. 15 (18 April).

Kuran, Timur. 2004. *Islam and Mammon: The Economic Predicaments of Islamism*. Princeton, NJ: Princeton University Press.

Lacey, Terry. 2009. "Islamic Finance: Why So Slow?" *Brunei Times* (5 March): www.bt.com.bn/en/analysis/2009/03/05/islamic_finance_why_so_slow.

Lerner, Michele. 2006. "Shariah Compliance Opens Doors for Islamic REITs." *Real Estate Portfolio* (September/October): www.realestateportfolio.com/portfoliomag/06sepoct/international.shtml.

Lim, Mohd Willieuddin. 2008. "Malaysia as a Hub for Islamic Wealth Management." CIMB Islamic, paper presented at the International Financial Planning Advisors Conference 2008.

Mahmood, Ahmed. 2004. "Islamic versus Traditional Banking in Arab Region: Premises and Promises." Paper submitted to the international seminar on "The Prospect of Arab Economic Cooperation" in Alexandria, Egypt (16–18 June).

Mansor, Asharul Huzairi Mohd. 2008. "Shariah Stock Screening Methodology: Defying the Leniency Allegation." *MIF Monthly* (July):30–31.

"Medical & Health Takaful." 2007. Insurance Info (www.insuranceinfo.com.my/choose_your_takaful/cover_your_health/medical_health_takaful.php?intPrefLangID=1).

Meezan Bank. 2008. "Project Financing, Expansion or BMR Requirement Solutions for Medium and Long Term Financing Requirements" (www.meezanbank.com/corp-pfe.aspx).

Mittal, Nisha. 2008. "Opalesque Launches New International Key Publication on Islamic Finance." Free Press Release (1 December): www.free-press-release.com/news/200812/1228111847.html.

Morais, Richard C. 2007. "Shariah Compliant Investments Don't Call It Interest." America2030.com 2007 Investor's Guide (23 July).

"Morgan Stanley Says Islamic Financial Assets to Go over $1 Trillion by 2010." 2008. *Shariah Finance Watch* (13 September): www.shariahfinancewatch.org/blog/2008/09/13/morgan-stanley-says-islamic-financial-assets-to-go-over-1-trillion-by-2010/.

Murugiah, S. 2007. "Half of Muslims to Deposit Money in Islamic Banks by 2015." *Edge Daily* (5 September): www.ibfim.com/images/kmc/PDF/half%20of.pdf.

Mustapha, N.H., and S.M.S. Salleh. 2002. "Corporate Governance from the Islamic Perspective." Institute of Islamic Understanding Malaysia, Kuala Lumpur, Malaysia.

Nafis, Alam, and Bala Shanmugam. 2007. "Strong Regulatory Framework: A Vital Tool for Islamic Banking." *Islamic Finance News*, vol. 4, no. 5 (2 February).

Nambiar, Nitin. 2008. "Sukuk Market to Be Worth $200bn by 2010." Emirates Business 24|7 (27 February): http://1efinance.spaces.live.com/blog/cns!395385358190596A!449.entry.

Ngadimon, Md Nurdin. 2009. "Overview of the Malaysian Islamic Capital Market & Recent Developments." Special session on Islamic finance, Bank of Mauritius (21 May): http://bom.intnet.mu/pdf/About/speeches/IFSBPresentation/Dr.Md%20Nurdin%20Ngadimon-%20Special%20Session.pdf.

Nordin, M. 2002. "The Need for Reform of Laws, Regulations and Rules on Corporate Governance in Malaysia." In *Corporate Governance from the Islamic Perspective.* Kuala Lumpur, Malaysia: Institute of Islamic Understanding Malaysia.

Nyazee, Imran Ahsan Khan. 2002. Outlines of Islamic Jurisprudence. Islamabad, Pakistan: Center for Islamic Law & Legal Heritage.

Nyee, Racheal Lee Mei. 2009. "Islamic Finance in the Limelight." *Edge Daily Online* (17 February): www.ibfim.com/index.php?option=com_content&task=view&id=2124&Itemid=99.

Parker, Mushtak. 2008a. "FTSE Forecasts Huge Growth for Islamic Equity." *Arab News* (5 May): www.arabnews.com/?page=6&section=0&article=109586&d=5&m=5&y=2008.

———. 2008b. "Is Islamic Finance Market Ready for Hedge Funds?" *Arab News* (4 August): www.arabnews.com/?page=6&section=0&article=112377&d=4&m=8&y=2008.

Pirani, Azeem. 2007. "Takaful: An Introduction." Presentation from Pak Qatar Takaful Group, Karachi, Pakistan (13 July): www.pakqatar.com.pk/downloads/presentations/takaful-introduction.pdf.

Reorient Legal. No date. "Takaful and Retakaful Companies" (https://www.reorient.co.uk/pdfs/takaful_retakaful_companies.pdf).

Robinson, Karina. 2007. "Islamic Finance Is Seeing Spectacular Growth." Times Reader 2.0 (5 November): www.iht.com/articles/2007/11/05/business/bankcol06.php.

Rosenbaum, Eric. 2008. "New ETF Manager Files First Islamic ETF for U.S." *News in Focus* (10 December): www.indexuniverse.com/sections/newsinfocus/5046-new-etf-manager-files-first-islamic-etf-for-us.html.

Rosly, S.A. 2005. *Critical Issues on Islamic Banking and Financial Markets.* Kuala Lumpur, Malaysia: Dinamas Publishing.

Saleem, Muhammad. 2006. *Islamic Banking: A $300 Billion Deception.* Bloomington, IN: Xlibris Corporation.

Salim, Nora. 2006. "Wealth Management." *Islamic Finance News*, vol. 3, no. 42 (24 November).

Securities Commission. 2005. *Guidelines on Real Estate Investment Trusts.* Kuala Lumpur, Malaysia: Malaysia Securities Commission.

Shakur, Lumumba K. 2001. "The Vindication of the People of the Maghrib Concerning the Issue of *Sadl*" (14 April): www.masud.co.uk/ISLAM/misc/yadain.htm.

Shanmugam, B., and L. Gupta. 2007. "Islamic Banking: A Technical Perspective." *In the Black* (CPA Australia) vol. 77, no. 10 (November):62–65.

"Sharia Mortgage Market Continues to Grow." 2008. Your Mortgage and Remortgage (19 February): www.yourmortgage.co.uk/showPage.html?page=3625040.

Siddiqi, Mohammad Nejatullah. 2007. "Economics of Tawarruq: How Its *Mafasid* Overwhelm the *Masalih*." A position paper presented at the workshop Tawarruq: A Methodological Issue in Shari'a-Compliant Finance (1 February): www.siddiqi.com/mns/Economics_of_Tawarruq.pdf.

Stanley, Mark. 2008. "Implementing Corporate Governance for Islamic Finance." Finance Netwerk (22 January): www.financenetwerk.nl/files/articles/90.pdf.

Suharmoko, A. 2008. "House Endorses Islamic Banking Law." *Jakarta Post* (18 June).

Sukri, Mohd Herwan, and Mohammad Hussin. 2006. "Developments of Islamic Swaps in Malaysia." Azmi & Associates (November):39 (www.pbpress.com/controlPanel/download.php?id=72).

"Sukuk Issuance to Exceed US$20 Bln This Year." 2008. Bernama, Malaysian National News Agency (10 September): www.bernama.com/bernama/v5/newsindex.php?id=358236.

Suleiman, Nasser M. 2005. "Corporate Governance in Islamic Banks." Al-Bab (12 October): www.al-bab.com/arab/econ/nsbanks.htm.

"Takaful: A Market with Great Potential." 2006. *Gulf News* (16 September): http://archive.gulfnews.com/articles/06/09/16/10067709.html.

Tamadontas, M. 2002. "Islam Law and Political Control in Contemporary Iran." *Journal for the Scientific Study of Religion*, vol. 40, no. 2 (December):205–220.

Tayar, Essam Al. 2006. "Islamic Investment Funds and Their Role in Developing Savings." *Islamic Finance News Guide 2006*:70–71.

Usmani, Mufti Taqi. No date. "Principles of Shariah Governing Islamic Investment Funds." *Albalagh* (www.albalagh.net/Islamic_economics/finance.shtml).

Walid, Tamara. 2008. "Noor Goes Moor." *Arabian Business.com* (21 June): www.arabianbusiness.com/522472-noor-goes-moor.

Zineldin, Mosad. 1990. *The Economics of Money and Banking: A Theoretical and Empirical Study of Islamic Interest-Free Banking*. Stockholm, Sweden: Almqvist & Wiksell International.

Zinkin, John. 2008. Opening remarks at the Islamic Markets Programme Innovating for Growth, Securities Commission, Kuala Lumpur, Malaysia (7 July): http://sidc.com.my/media/speech/imp-welcome-remark-johnzinkin.html.

Additional Readings

Chapter 1

Ahmad, Ziauddin. 1984. "Framework of Islamic Banking." *Journal of Islamic Banking and Finance*, vol. 1, no. 2 (Spring).

Ali, A.M. 2002. "The State and Future of Islamic Banks on the World Economic Scene." Islamic Development Bank Staff Papers.

Ariff, M. 1988. "Islamic Banking." *Asian-Pacific Economic Literature*, vol. 2, no. 2 (September):48–64.

El-Gamal, Mahmoud. 2000. *A Basic Guide to Contemporary Islamic Banking and Finance*. Houston: Rice University.

Haron, S. 1997. *Islamic Banking: Rules and Regulations*. Petaling Jaya, Malaysia: Pelanduk Publications.

Haron, S., and B. Shanmugam. 2001. *Islamic Banking System: Concept and Applications*. Petaling Jaya, Malaysia: Pelanduk Publications.

Lewis, M.K., and L.M. Algaoud. 2001. *Islamic Banking*. Cheltenham, U.K.: Edward Elgar Publishing Ltd.

Muslehuddin, M. 1993. *Banking and Islamic Law*. New Delhi, India: Universal Offset Printers.

Radwan, Zeinab. 2006. "The Rights of Islam." *Al-Ahram Weekly On-Line*, no. 824 (14–20 December): http://weekly.ahram.org.eg/2006/824/sc16.htm.

Schaik, D.V. 2001. "Islamic Banking." *Arab Bank Review*, vol. 3, no. 1.

Shariff, Mohammed Ismail. 2005. "Salient Features of Islamic Banking Act, 1983 and Banking and Financial Institutions Act, 1989." Finance in Islam (www.financeinislam.com/article/6_31/1/197).

Shingeri, M.S. 1994. *A Model of Pure Interest-Free Banking*. New Delhi, India: Islamic Fiqh Academy.

Usmani, M.T. 2002. *An Introduction to Islamic Finance*. The Hague, Netherlands: Kluwer.

"Why Islam Has Prohibited Interest and Islamic Alternatives for Financing." 2005. First Ethical Ltd., Bolton, United Kingdom. Accessed on 10 March 2009 at http://msmsoton.files.wordpress.com/2008/02/guide-to-interest.pdf.

Chapter 2

Al-Qari, Abdul Aziz. 1998. "The Importance of Aqidah." Salafi Publications (10 June): www.sahihalbukhari.com/sps/sp.cfm?subsecID=AQD01&articleID=AQD010001&articlePages=1.

Al-'Ujaji, Walid b. Ibrahim. "Qiyas in Islamic Law—A Brief Introduction." Islam Today (www.islamtoday.com/showme2.cfm?cat_id=2&sub_cat_id=1284).

Ayaz, Maryam. 2009. "Overview of Islamic Banking." Apvision International (www.apvision.com.pk/islamic_banking_finance_economics.html).

Baianonie, Imam Mohamed. 1987. "Islam Declared Equality among People." Speech delivered at the Islamic Center of Raleigh, NC (20 February): http://islam1.org/khutub/Equal.among_People.htm.

Billah, Mohd. Ma'sum. 2001. "Sources of Law Affecting *Takaful* (Islamic Insurance)." *International Journal of Islamic Financial Services*, vol. 2. no. 4.

———. 2003. *Modern Financial Transactions under Syariah*. Selangor, Malaysia: Ilmiah Publications.

Bin Abdullah, Mohd Asri. 2005. "Being a Good Muslim and Its Relation to Corporate Social Responsibility." Department of Islamic Development Malaysia (JAKIM) (17 October): www.islam.gov.my/portal/lihat.php?jakim=703.

Haddad, G.F. No date. "The Meaning of Sunnah" (http://sunnah.org/fiqh/usul/meaning_sunnah.htm).

"Islamic Economics" (www.islamic-world.net/economics/contract.htm).

Islamic-World.Net: Official Website of Khalifah Institute (www.islamic-world.net).

"Istihsan and Maslaha." 2002. Witness-Pioneer International (www.witness-pioneer.org/vil/Books/SH_Usul/istihsan_and_maslaha.htm).

"Public Interest (*Maslahah*)." 2003. Islam Online (16 January): www.islamonline.net/servlet/Satellite?cid=1119503543654&pagename=IslamOnline-English-Ask_Scholar%2FFatwaE%2FPrintFatwaE.

Thomas, Abdulkader, Stella Cox, and Bryan Kraty, eds. 2005. *Structuring Islamic Finance Transactions*. London: Euromoney Books.

"What Is Sunnah?" 1997. *Invitation to Islam* (September): www.islaamnet.com.

Chapter 3

Gafoor, A.L.M. Abdul. 1999. "Islamic Banking and Finance: Another Approach." Revised version of paper presented at the Islamic Hinterland Conference on Critical Debates among Canadian Muslims, Toronto (3–5 September): http://users.bart.nl/~abdul/book4ft.html.

Hameed, Tariq. 2007. "Diminishing Musharaka Reflects the Spirit of Sharia." ShariaBanking.net (5 January): http://global.shariabanking.net/islamic-equity/diminishing-musharaka-reflects-the-spirit-of-s-8.html.

Hasan, Zubair. 2008. "Credit Creation and Control: An Unresolved Issue in Islamic Banking." *International Journal of Islamic and Middle Eastern Finance and Management*, vol. 1, no. 1:69–81.

"Islamic Banking Deposits in UAE Hit $20bn." 2008. The Islamic Finance Blog (May 13): http://islamicfinancenews.wordpress.com/2008/05/13/islamic-banking-deposits-in-uae-hit-20bn.

Khan, M. Mansoor, and M. Ishaq Bhatti. 2008. "Islamic Banking and Finance: On Its Way to Globalization." *Managerial Finance*, vol. 34, no. 10:708–725.

"Liberty Is Still High on the Agenda." 1999. *Milli Gazette, Turkey* (Interview with Abdelwahab El-Affendi): www.witness-pioneer.org/vil/Articles/shariah/liberty_still_high_on_agenda.htm.

Memon, Noor Ahmed. 2007. "Islamic Banking: Present and Future Challenges." *Journal of Management and Social Sciences*, vol. 3, no. 1 (Spring):1–10.

Parker, Mushtak. 2008. "EFH to Operate as Islamic Investment Bank in UK." *Arab News* (12 March): www.arabnews.com/?page=6&section=0&article=107742&d=12&m=3&y=2008.

Wilson, Rodney. 2008. "Islamic Finance in Europe." *Islamic Finance News*, vol. 5, no. 10 (14 March).

Chapter 4

Alhabshi, Syed Othman. 1994. "Development of Capital Market under Islamic Principles." Paper presented at the 1994 Conference on Managing and Implementing Interest-Free Banking/Islamic Financial System, Centre for Management Technology, Kuala Lumpur, Malaysia (25–26 January).

Anwar, Zarinah. 2005. "A Strong and Vibrant Financial Sector for Sustainable Growth—The Role of Capital Markets." 30th Annual Meeting of the Islamic Development Bank.

Archer, Simon. 2008. "An Overview of Islamic Capital Markets and Issues in their Development." IFSB Islamic Capital Market Seminar, Male, Maldives (24 January).

Bach, Obiyathulla Ismath. No date. "Derivatives in Islamic Finance—An Overview." International Islamic University, Malaysia.

"Derivatives in Islamic Finance." 2008. *Islamic Finance News*, vol. 5, no. 23 (13 June).

"ETFs All the Rage in Equity Market." 2008. *Islamic Finance News*, vol. 5, no. 14 (11 April).

"Examples of Sukuk Issuances and Their Structures." 2008. Sukuk.net (7 June): www.sukuk.net/news/newsfull.php?newid=6100.

"Getting over the Misconceptions of Islamic Unit Trusts." 2007. *Islamic Finance News*, vol. 4, no. 6 (9 February).

Grewal, Baljeet Kaur. 2007. "Islamic Capital Market Growth and Trends." *Islamic Finance News Guide 2007*:29–32.

Hasan, S.U. 2005. "Islamic Unit Trusts." *Finance in Islam* (www.financeinislam.com/article/1_35/17/277).

"The Islamic Capital Market." No date. Bursa Malaysia (www.klse.com.my/website/bm/products_and_services/information_services/downloads/bm2ICM.pdf).

"Islamic Capital Market." No date. Malaysia Securities Commision (www.sc.com.my/sub.asp?pageid=&menuid=267&newsid=&linkid=&type=).

"Islamic Capital Market Fact Finding Report." 2004. Islamic Capital Market Task Force of the International Organization of Securities Commissions (July): www.iiibf.org/media/ICM-IOSCOFactfindingReport.pdf.

"Islamic Indices—The Way Forward." 2008. *Islamic Finance News*, vol. 5, no. 25 (27 June).

Khan, Iqbal. 2005. "Liquidity Management of Islamic Financial Institutions in the UAE." Central Bank of UAE, Abu Dhabi, UAE.

Othman, Jal. 2006. "Raising Capital through Labuan IOFC." At the Labuan IOFC Conference on The Investment Route to Asia.

"An Overview of Sukuk." Sukuk.net (http://sukuk.net/news/newsfull.php?newid=6097).

Quarterly Bulletin of Malaysian Islamic Capital Market. Various issues. Malaysia Securities Commission (www.sc.com.my/main.asp?pageid=250&menuid=269&newsid=&linkid=&type=).

"S&P Pioneers Investible Shari'ah." 2008. *Financial Express* (19 February): www.financialexpress.com/news/S&P-pioneers-investible-Shariah-indices/274781.

Wilson, Rodney. 2007. "Global Islamic Capital Markets: Review of 2006 and Prospects for 2007." SGIA Research Working Paper Series (June): www.dur.ac.uk/resources/sgia/SGIARWP07-05.pdf.

Zahari, Juniza. 2006. "A Rating Perspective of Sukuk Musharakah Transactions." *Islamic Finance News Guide 2006*:64–66.

Chapter 5

"Abu Dhabi Sees Potential in Islamic Insurance." 2007. Oxford Business Group (1 March). Available at *Arabian Business.com* (www.arabianbusiness.com/10037-dhabi-sees-potential-in-islamic-insurance).

Ebrahim, M. Shahid, and Tan Kai Joo. 2001. "Islamic Banking in Brunei Darussalam." *International Journal of Social Economics*, vol. 28, no. 4:314–337.

"Family Takaful." 2007. Insurance Info (www.insuranceinfo.com.my/_system/media/downloadables/family_takaful.pdf).

"Family Takaful: Case for 'Window' Operations." 2006. SEPC Life Insurance Workshop (14 September): www.secp.gov.pk/Events/pdf/FamilyTakaful_MohammedAli.pdf.

Fisher, Omar, and Dawood Y. Taylor. 2000. "Prospects for Evolution of Takaful in the 21st Century." Bank Aljazira (April): www.takaful.com.sa/m4sub3.asp.

"Islamic Insurance Firm to Begin Working Soon." 2006. *Daily Times* (13 December): www.dailytimes.com.pk/default.asp?page=2006%5C12%5C13% 5Cstory_13-12-2006_pg5_7.

Khan, M. Jamil Akhtar. 2006. "Takaful: An Emerging Niche Market." Presentation to seminar held by the Institute of Chartered Accountants of Pakistan (19 October).

Mangi, Naween A. "Emirates Investment to Sell Islamic Insurance in Pakistan." *Bloomberg.com* (30 November): www.bloombergl.com/apps/news?pid=20601091&sid=aaizDhH4VD.k&refer=india.

"Takaful Concept in Family Takaful." 2007. Cottage Industry and Islamic Insurance (2 October): http://eynotrading.blogspot.com/2007/10/takaful-concept-in-family-takaful.html.

Chapter 6

Al-Fil, Gérard. 2008. "Despite Its Growth Islamic Finance Faces Obstacles." AME Info (3 June): www.ameinfo.com/159020.html.

———. 2008. "Shariah-Compliant Commodity Trading Gathers Pace in Dubai." AME Info (21 May): www.ameinfo.com/157605.html.

"Al-Hadharah, the Real McCoy of I-REITs." 2008. *Islamic Finance News*, vol. 5, no. 1 (11 January).

Al-Rifa, Tariq. 2003. "An Overview of Islamic Finance and the Growth of Islamic Funds." Paper presented at the Islamic Equity Funds Workshop, Kuala Lumpur, Malaysia.

Banerjee, Alka. 2008. "Pessimism Persists in Global Property and REITs." *Islamic Finance News*, vol. 5, no. 18 (9 May).

Bescht, Catharina-Sophie. 2007. "Islamic Private Equity Outgrowing Conventional." *Islamic Finance News*, vol. 4, no. 24 (15 June).

"Channelling Liquidity into Islamic Finance." 2007. Paper presented at the Global Islamic Finance Forum, Malaysia (March): www.bnm.gov.my/microsites/giff2007/pdf/iif/Session4_d2.pdf.

CIMB Islamic. 2008. "CIMB-Principal Rides on Strong Global Commodities Outlook" (21 April): www.cimbislamic.com/index.php?ch=islam_about_news&pg=islam_about_news_oview&ac=1285&tpt=islamic.

Hanware, Khalil. 2006. "How Have Islamic Funds Performed?" *Arab News* (6 February): www.arabnews.com/?page=6&section=0&article=77400&d=6&m=2&y=2006.

Hunt, Laalitha. 2008. "Bullish Outlook for Commodities." *Star Online* (20 May): http://biz.thestar.com.my/news/story.asp?file=/2008/5/20/business/21299725&sec=business.

Institute of Islamic Banking and Insurance. No date. "Islamic Banking: Islamic Equity Funds" (www.islamic-banking.com/ibanking/ief.php).

Islamic Capital Market, Securities Commission Malaysia. No date. "Islamic REITs: Growth and Opportunities." *MIF Monthly* (www.mifmonthly.com/article9.php).

"Islamic Real Estate Investment Trusts (REITs)." 2007. *Islamic Finance News*. Bahrain Report (31 August).

Jaffer, Sohail. No date. "Islamic Wealth Management." *Islamic Business and Finance*, no. 58. Reprinted from *Islamic Finance Newsletter* of February 2005: www.cpifinancial.net/v2/print.aspx?pg=magazine&aid=912.

Johnson, Douglas Clark. 2007. "Islamic Asset Management: Beyond the Thobe." Calyx Financial (31 October): www.failaka.com/downloads/Johnson_BeyondtheThobe103107.pdf.

Juma, Yousif A. 2007. "Islamic Wealth Management." *Islamic Finance News Guide 2007*:67–68.

Merhi, Samer. 2008. "Comparison of REITs and I-REITs." *Islamic Finance News Asset & Wealth Management Guide 2008* (http://islamicfinancenews.com/supplement_2008_a&w.asp).

Miller, Neil D., Dean Naumowicz, and Aziza Atta. 2008. "Investing in Islamic Structured Products." *Islamic Finance News Guide 2008*:33–36.

Mokhtar, Shabnam. 2008. "Will Writing: A New Retail Product in Malaysia." *Islamic Finance News*, vol. 5, no. 24 (20 June).

Shariff, Mohamed Ismail. 2007. "Legal and Legislative Issues in I-REITs." *Islamic Finance News*, vol. 4, no. 47 (23 November).

Siddiqi, Moin A. 2004. "Islamic Investment." *Middle East* (May): http://findarticles.com/p/articles/mi_m2742/is_345/ai_n25094793/print?tag=artBody;col1.

Smyth, Mark J. 2006. "Islamic Funds Come of Age." *Middle East Banker*:28–30 (www.failaka.com/downloads/Nov06_BME%20islamic%20funds.pdf).

Stanton, Daniel. 2008. "Islamic Equity Funds See Rapid Growth." *Arabian Business.com* (18 February): www.arabianbusiness.com/511518-islamic-equity-funds-see-rapid-growth.

Wilson, Ted. 2008. "Growing Appetite for Islamic Wealth." *Professional Wealth Management* (1 May): www.pwmnet.com/news/fullstory.php/aid/2241/Growing_appetite_for_Islamic_wealth_.html.

Yousaf, Khalid. 2007. "Exploring Growth Opportunities in Wealth Management." Paper presented at the Global Islamic Finance Forum, Kuala Lumpur, Malaysia (March): www.bnm.gov.my/microsites/giff2007/pdf/iif/Session3_c.pdf.

Chapter 7

"AAOIFI Shariah Council's Proposals for Amendments in Contemporary Sukuk Issues." 2008. Islamic Finance Blog (21 May): http://islamicfinancenews.wordpress.com/2008/05/21/aaoifi-shariah-councils-proposals-for-amendments-in-contemporary-sukuk-issues.

Abdullah, Daud. 2005. "Shariah Compliance Reviews." *Islamic Finance News*, vol. 2, no. 8 (18 April).

Ahmad, Jameel. 2007. "Role of Standards-Setting Bodies in Promoting Shari'a-Compliant Deposit Insurance System." Paper presented at the Sixth International Association of Deposit Insurers Conference, Kuala Lumpur, Malaysia.

Akhta, Shamshad. 2006. "Shari'a Compliant Corporate Governance." Keynote address by the Governor of the State Bank of Pakistan at the annual Corporate Governance Conference, Dubai, United Arab Emirates.

Asri, Mohamed, and Mohamed Fahmi. 2003–2004. "Contribution of the Islamic Worldview towards Corporate Governance." Master of Science in Accounting Sem 2 2003/04 (www.iiu.edu.my/iaw/Students%20Term%20Papers_files/Asri%20and%20Fahmi%20IslWWandCG.htm).

Aziz, Zeti Akhtar. 2004. "Approaches to Regulation of Islamic Financial Services Industry." Governor's speech at the IFSB Summit on Islamic Financial Services Industry and the Global Regulatory Environment, London (18 May): www.bnm.gov.my/index.php?ch=9&pg=15&ac=151.

Bank Negara Malaysia. 2005. "The Rise and Effectiveness of Corporate Governance in the Islamic Financial Services Industry." Governor's speech at the Second IFSB Summit, Doha, Qatar (24 May): www.bnm.gov.my/index.php?ch=9&pg=15&ac=170.

Bank of New York Mellon. No date. "Improving Corporate Governance in Islamic Finance." Innovation Series: Global Corporate Trust (www.bankofny.com/CpTrust/data/tl_islamic_finance.pdf).

Capulong, Ma Virginita, David Edwards, David Webb, and Juzhong Zhuang, eds. 2000. *Corporate Governance and Finance in East Asia: A Study of Indonesia, Republic of Korea, Malaysia, Philippines, and Thailand: Volume One (A Consolidated Report)*. Manila, Philippines: Asian Development Bank (http://adb.org/Documents/Books/Corporate_Governance/Vol1/default.asp).

Chapra, M. Umer, and Habib Ahmed. 2002. *Corporate Governance in Islamic Financial Institutions*. Jeddah, Saudi Arabia: Islamic Development Bank.

Cunningham, Andrew. 2004. "Regulation and Supervision: Challenges for Islamic Finance in a Riba-Based Global System." Moody's Special Comment, Report No. 81128, Moody's Investors Service (January).

Dar, Humayon. 2005. "Islamic Banks: Are They Really What Their Stakeholders Intended Them to Be?" *Islamic Finance News*, vol. 2, no. 13 (27 June).

El Qorchi, Mohammed. 2005. "Islamic Finance Gears Up." *Finance and Development*, vol. 42, no. 4 (December): www.imf.org/external/pubs/ft/fandd/2005/12/qorchi.htm.

Federal Home Loan Bank of Boston. No date. "Corporate Governance Principles" (www.fhlbboston.com/aboutus/thebank/08_01_10_corporate_governance_principles.jsp).

Grais, Wafik, and Matteo Pellegrini. 2006. "Corporate Governance and Shariah Compliance." *Islamic Finance News*, vol. 3, no. 45 (15 December).

Ibrahim, Ali A. 2006. "Convergence of Corporate Governance and Islamic Financial Services Industry: Toward Islamic Financial Services Securities Market." Georgetown Law Graduate Paper Series: http://lsr.nellco.org/cgi/viewcontent.cgi?article=1002&context=georgetown/gps.

"Islamic Finance Meets in Malaysia." No date. Malaysia International Islamic Financial Centre (www.mifc.com/index.php?ch=cat_int_isbank&pg=cat_int_isbank_val#).

Kadir, Mohd Razif Abdul. 2007. "International Regulatory Standards for Islamic Finance: Implementation Issues and Challenges." Paper presented at the Global Islamic Finance Forum, Kuala Lumpur, Malaysia (28 March).

Kadir, Mohd Razif bin Abd. 2006. "Malaysia's Position as an International Islamic Financial Centre." Closing address by the deputy governor of the Central Bank of Malaysia at the Malaysian Islamic Finance: Issuers and Investors Forum, Kuala Lumpur, Malaysia (15 August): www.bis.org/review/r060825f.pdf.

Knight, Malcolm D. 2007. "The Growing Importance of Islamic Finance in the Global Financial System." Paper presented at the Second Islamic Financial Services Board Forum, Frankfurt (6 December): www.bis.org/speeches/sp071210.htm.

"Meet the Head." 2006. *Islamic Finance News*, vol. 3, no. 27 (11 August).

PricewaterhouseCoopers. No date. "Regulatory Review of Islamic Finance in Malaysia." *MIF Monthly* (www.mifmonthly.com/article10.php).

Rowey, Kent, Charles July, and Marc Fèvre. 2006. "Islamic Finance: Basic Principles and Structures: A Focus on Project Finance." Freshfields Bruckhaus Deringer (January): www.freshfields.com/publications/pdfs/2006/13205.pdf.

Ruin, Joseph Eby. 2004. "Instilling Risk Management Culture for Corporate Governance in Islamic Banking." *Islamic Finance News*, vol. 1, no. 2.

Sulaeiman, M. Nasser. No date. "Corporate Governance in Islamic Banks." *Islamic Economics* (http://islamic-world.net/economics/corporate_gov.htm).

Wouters, Paul. 2005. "Compliance and Compliance Function." *Islamic Finance News*, vol. 2, no. 22 (7 November).

Zaidi, Jamal Abbas. 2006. "Rating of Islamic Banks and Financial Institutions." Paper presented at the 13th World Islamic Banking Conference, Bahrain (9 December): www.iirating.com/presentation/20061209_rating_of_islamic_banks_and_financial_institutions.pdf.

Chapter 8

Ahmed, Elwaleed M. 2007. "There May Be Trouble Ahead." *Zawya.com* (May/June): www.zawya.com/story.cfm/sidZAWYA20070614061339.

————. No date. "Challenges Facing Sector's Growth; Global Islamic Finance." *Sudaneseeconomist.com*: http://sudaneseeconomist.com/islam_1.html.

"Bahraini Banking and Finance Sectors in Shipshape." 2008. *Bahrain Tribune* (4 August): www.menafn.com/qn_news_story_s.asp?StoryId=1093206647.

Hassan, Eman. 2008. "Middle East Poised to Invest in Turkey." AME Info (17 August): www.ameinfo.com/166321.html.

©2009 The Research Foundation of CFA Institute

"Islamic Banks Face Obstacles Even in Islamic Countries." 2008. MEMRI Economic Blog (8 February): http://memrieconomicblog.org/bin/content.cgi?news=1062.

"Islamic Finance Industry." 2005. Academy for International Modern Studies (reprinted from *Washington Times* of 21 March 2000): http://learnislamicfinance.com/Islamic-Finance-Industry.htm.

Kapur, Shuchita. 2008. "Islamic Banking Is Going Mainstream." *RIBH—Le Journal de la Finance Islamique* (29 April): http://ribh.wordpress.com/2008/04/29/islamic-banking-is-going-mainstream.

Poole, Ben. 2007. "Growth and Diversification in Islamic Finance." gtnews.com (25 July): www.gtnews.com/feature/196.cfm.

Remo-Listana, Karen. 2008. "Standardisation Has to Wait." Emirates Business 24|7 (21 September): www.business24-7.ae/articles/2008/9/pages/09212008_69ecefe8f0bd4ed5a0e7064194eb511f.aspx.

Rohde, Peter. 2008. "Islamic Banking." Peter Rohde's Blog (24 July): http://peterrohde.wordpress.com/2008/07/24/islamic-banking.

State Bank of Pakistan. 2007. "Process for Standardization of Shariah Practices" (7 August): www.sbp.org.pk/ibd/2007/Shariah-Practices-07-Aug-07.pdf.

Suharmoko, Aditya. 2008. "House Endorses Islamic Bank Law." *Jakarta Post* (18 June): www.thejakartapost.com/news/2008/06/18/house-endorses-islamic-bank-law.html.

Tamadonfar, Mehran. 2001. "Islam, Law and Political Control in Contemporary Iran." *Journal for the Scientific Study of Religion*, vol. 40, no. 2 (June):205–220.

Wouters, Paul. 2008. "Update on Participation Banking in Turkey: 2008." Grandstanding Traction (first published in *Islamic Finance News*, 18 April 2008): http://grandstandingtraction.blogspot.com/2008/06/update-on-participation-banking-in.html.

Zaidi, Jamal Abbas. 2008. "Developing Islamic Financial Markets for Investors." Paper presented at the Arab Banking Conference 2008, Cairo, Egypt (6–7 April): www.iirating.com/presentation/arab_banking_conference_2008.pdf.